The GLASS ARTIST'S

STUDIO HANDBOOK

QUARRY

BEVERLY MASSACHUSETTS

The GLASS ARTIST'S
STUDIO HANDBOOK

Traditional and
Contemporary Techniques
for Working with Glass

QUARRY BOOKS

Cecilia Cohen

Text © 2011 by Cecilia Cohen
Photography and Design © 2011 Quarry Books

First published in the United States of America in 2011 by
Quarry Books, a member of
Quayside Publishing Group
100 Cummings Center
Suite 406-L
Beverly, Massachusetts 01915-6101
Telephone: (978) 282-9590
Fax: (978) 283-2742
www.quarrybooks.com
Visit www.Craftside.Typepad.com for a behind-the-scenes peek at our crafty world!

10 9 8 7 6 5 4 3 2 1

ISBN-13: 978-1-59253-697-9
ISBN-10: 1-59253-697-2

Digital edition published in 2011
eISBN-13: 978-1-61058-026-7

Library of Congress Cataloging-in-Publication Data available

Design: Laura H. Couallier, Laura Herrmann Design
Cover Images: Nataly Cohen Kadosh, except top-middle, Kerri Fuhr,
                and middle-left, Aimee Mitchell
Photography: Nataly Cohen Kadosh

Printed in China

For My Sons

Efi, Asaf, Nadav, and Daniel
because, in the end, it's all about love.

Contents

Recycled Bottle Necklace,
page 125

Tea Light Dish,
page 90

Introduction

GLASS IS WONDERFUL. When declared with feeling, this statement expresses the intense passion that I feel for my craft. It is, however, a woefully inadequate way to start a book about glass art techniques; it expresses neither the joy and opportunities for creative expression and satisfaction that can be gained from creating glass art, nor the time, effort, and commitment that we must give to learn techniques, develop designs, and create a unique piece. The challenge is always there: When we start and when we finish, glass is hard and stiff. It's only when we are working with glass that we can cut it, melt it, shape it, arrange it, and manipulate it. Many times, it's an unforgiving material. Yet the beauty in glass has captured hearts and hands for thousands of years. While glass art techniques were once trade secrets, jealously kept within families, today the materials, tools, and training are easily within reach of almost anyone interested in learning the craft. We can create pieces that are extraordinarily useful or simply decorative, of almost any size. Glass, I believe, has something for everyone.

Is This Book for You?

If you're interested in learning glass art techniques, if you have some techniques under your belt and wish to learn more, or if you're looking for one definitive "bible" for the three techniques covered on these pages, this handbook is right for you.

In part 1 of *The Glass Artist's Studio Handbook,* we'll cover the basics of setting up a studio, including guidelines for working safely, and we'll provide an overview of common tools and supplies. In part 2, we'll explore three popular techniques for creating glass art. In part 3, we'll combine those techniques to create unique projects that will challenge you and advance your skills.

Hopefully, even if you're already familiar with many of the subjects covered, this book will add to your proficiency and stimulate you to think about design and technique in new ways that you'll ultimately express in your creations.

Starting from Scratch:
Setting Up
Your Studio

Planning the
Studio Layout

Studio Infrastructure

Designing a glass art studio is a bit like designing a kitchen, in that you must consider plumbing, electrical needs, storage, lighting, ventilation, workstations, and traffic flow (where you and others will walk and stand when not at a workstation). Few of us are blessed with unlimited space and funds, and most of us plan our studio around preexisting constraints such as room dimensions, water pipes, electrical outlets, and windows. Common infrastructure issues that every studio artist must take into account include the following:

Lighting: Without adequate light, you'll see colors incorrectly, make more technical errors, and be more likely to have an accident. If you can't move or improve your lighting, move your workstations to the best-lit areas in your studio.

Electrical needs: Many tools require electricity; add more outlets than you think you'll need. Include at least one protected outlet near your sink for a glass grinder. Some heavy equipment, such as a fusing kiln, requires heavier-than-house current with special outlets that must be installed by an electrician.

LEFT A variety of hand tools are used to cut and manipulate glass. We'll discuss tools and supplies in-depth in chapter 2.

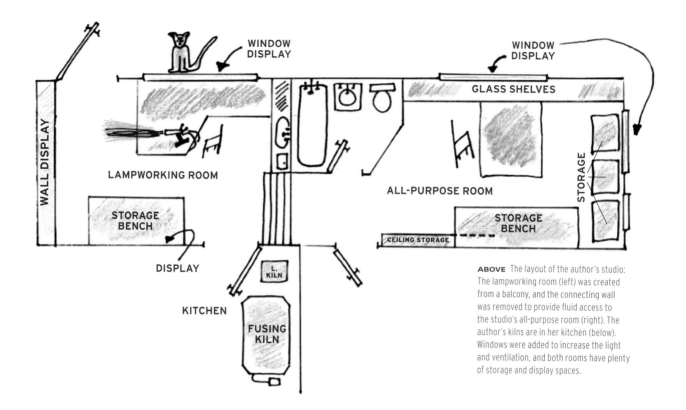

WINDOW DISPLAY

WINDOW DISPLAY

GLASS SHELVES

WALL DISPLAY

LAMPWORKING ROOM

ALL-PURPOSE ROOM

STORAGE

STORAGE BENCH

DISPLAY

STORAGE BENCH

CEILING STORAGE

L. KILN

KITCHEN

FUSING KILN

ABOVE The layout of the author's studio: The lampworking room (left) was created from a balcony, and the connecting wall was removed to provide fluid access to the studio's all-purpose room (right). The author's kilns are in her kitchen (below). Windows were added to increase the light and ventilation, and both rooms have plenty of storage and display spaces.

Water: Most glass work requires water; a sink is a very handy thing to have in your studio. You'll want to clean your pieces in progress and when finished. You'll need to wash your hands before you leave your studio for any reason. You'll need fresh water to prepare mosaic grout, bead release, and kiln wash, and to top off your glass grinder. You should not use your kitchen sink for any of these tasks.

Ventilation: All glass work requires ventilation, and an open window is usually not enough. A fume hood, such as a kitchen hood, can be installed over your workstations. Place a small tabletop fume trap next to your soldering iron and a large tabletop fan in the window, facing outward, to suck dirty air from the room and blow it outside. Lampworking needs intense ventilation because as we heat glass in the flame, metals and other materials are released from the glass. Fusing kilns can stink as they heat up, and you'll wish you had better ventilation although, as a rule, the smell isn't indicative of danger or a threat to your health.

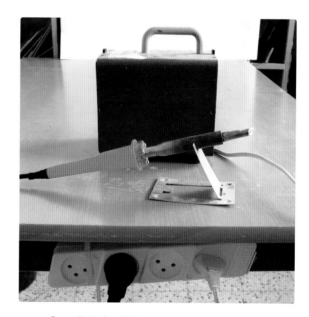

ABOVE For smaller tools and table lamps, install outlet strips with on/off switches so that you can easily turn on several items simultaneously, such as a soldering iron and a portable fume trap; it's easy to remember that the soldering iron is still on when you hear the whirr of the trap's fan, and you won't forget to turn on the fume trap before soldering.

Planning the Work Area

There's no such thing as a perfect studio. Your goal should be how to best fit what you require into what you already have or can achieve with minimal renovations. It's always a good idea to have extra space for future expansion.

WORKSTATIONS

Workstation is an all-purpose word for a collection of furniture and tools that support a particular activity.

A **wet station** is the spot where you'll stand to do all your wet work—no chair is needed. It should have a sink, and counter space for a glass grinder and small items such as old toothbrushes and soaps. A grinder tends to spray water with fine bits of ground glass, so don't put the wet station in the middle of the display gallery.

TIP | **When It's Just Not Possible...**

If you haven't the room or budget to set up a glass art studio, don't despair. Some schools and craft centers open their studios for students and hobbyists; a few of the best known are listed in this book's "Resources" section. Many artists teach and some artists rent out studio space. If you like an artist's work, or if the artist is conveniently located nearby, ask if he or she offers such arrangements. A quick search on the Internet should help you find opportunities in your area.

Setting two worktables in an *L* shape lets you move easily from one workstation to the next as you work on your projects.

This torch station sits at the window, where natural light streams through the glass rods and shows off their true colors.

Conserving Water

Making glass art (particularly stained glass) requires a lot of water. Projects must be frequently washed between steps, but it isn't necessary to use clean water every time. Place a basin in your sink and a small open container of clean water on the countertop. Wash your work in the basin and rinse it in the container. When you feel you absolutely must have clean, flowing water, the basin will catch it for later use. Sometimes pieces can be wiped clean with a soapy cloth, rinsed in the basin, and then rinsed in the container. The same basin water can be used for soaking beads and reaming them to remove bead release (with a rinse in the clean water), washing stained glass, and cleaning fused pieces. When the basin water becomes murky, pour it out at the base of a tree. When the container water is no longer clean, pour it into the basin.

Near your sink you'll need a **drying station,** a surface where you dry things, such as the glass that was just ground at the wet station or beads that you just cleaned in the sink. My drying station is conveniently equipped with a plastic dish rack and a garbage can under the sink.

For all the techniques taught in this handbook except lampworking, you'll need a **glass cutting station.** Cutting stations have a flat surface covered with a cutting pad, a glass cutter in a jar with cutting oil, some permanent ink pens, and tools such as rulers, ring stars/blue runners, and pattern shears.

You'll need a **prep station** where you draw patterns, wrap copper foil, sort through frit and fusing glass scraps, string jewelry, and glue mosaics. You might also photograph your work here if the lighting is appropriate. One note of caution: If your studio contains glass of more than one type, you must clear this table well between tasks or you'll run the risk of mixing glass families. Even a small mix of glass families in a hot or warm technique will ruin a fused piece or a lampwork bead.

Ideally you'll have a unique **soldering station,** with a wooden surface (where you'll solder stained glass pieces and superheat metal wires), a soldering iron and its metal stand, a wet rag for cleaning the soldering iron as you work, a fume trap, a small dish of flux, and a flux brush. You'll want to sit while performing most of these tasks, so include a chair.

The **torch station** will be the center of lampworking activities. This station requires a heat-proof surface (either part of the table's construction or added on top). The torch must be affixed to the tabletop, and you'll rest your tools and glass rods on the station top. I work sitting down, so I recommend a chair for this station. Also, take into account the direction of the torch flame when situating your torch station; the flame will stretch from the torch, over the table, and beyond. If your studio is very small, you might want to heat-proof the opposite wall. (You'll find more about setting up your torch station in chapter 2.)

SPECIAL LAYOUT CONSIDERATIONS

- **Bathrooms:** A studio shower or bathtub is advantageous if you make large stained glass pieces such as windows, but a garden hose outdoors works just as well in many climates.
- **Fire hazards:** Fire hazards are inherent in several glass art processes. Beading kilns, fusing kilns, and torch flames must be kept away from all combustibles, including furniture. Kilns must be placed a minimal distance from walls, a distance determined by the manufacturers. The location of the kilns will directly affect the level of safety for you, your students, your visitors, and your family.
- **Eat, drink, and be merry:** But not in your work area. If it's important to you, include a refreshment station in your clean, work-free display gallery.
- **Legal considerations:** Your local council, business license, or insurance may require that you fulfill certain conditions to meet the law or receive coverage. Research the requirements that apply to your studio so that you can include them in your plans.

The torch is placed in the center of this station, and the surfaces and walls in front of it have been heat-proofed with metal sheeting.

Safety Alerts!

TORCH SAFETY

The torch flame is fed by a steady flow of gas and oxygen. If your gas and/or oxygen supply comes from cylinders, they should be stored outside, for safety's sake. Regulations often require that the cylinders be chained to the wall or enclosed in a way that prevents them from being knocked over. Check the requirements for your location.

KILN SAFETY

Kilns are built to contain heat, not to release heat into the room. However, some heat does escape, and for this reason kilns should always be placed in a fireproof area of your studio. To protect electrical components and digital controllers, kilns should be indoors, not outdoors exposed to the weather. No matter what size your kiln or what use you'll be putting it to, before firing up your kiln you must always check around, under, and over your kiln to be sure you haven't forgotten anything combustible nearby. Your kiln will run for seven to fifteen hours per firing, so it will get hot—and stay hot—for long enough to melt or ignite even the most stubborn of papers, cardboard, plastics, or wooden objects.

Storage

STORING GLASS

Art glass for stained glass and mosaics can be stored together and sorted by color, size, or any other system that makes sense to you. If you're practicing fusing or lampworking, *all* the glass in your studio must be carefully separated by glass family (referred to as COE), separate from the mosaic/stained glass art glass. Warm and hot glass families are assigned numbers that reflect their viscosity (think sticky toffee) and spread (think flowing lava). Common families for fusing are COE 90 and COE 96, while many flameworkers prefer COE 104. COE is covered further throughout this handbook. The most important thing is that *different glass families cannot be mixed.* Each family, therefore, requires separate, clearly marked storage. Once you mix them up, they must all be downgraded to stained glass/mosaic art glass because it's usually impossible to identify a glass's family by appearance only. Distinct storage areas for different types of glass are not a "nice to have," but a "must have"!

No matter what glass family or type you're working with, sheets of glass are best stored in small groups standing on edge. Bins work well for scraps. Visit your local artists, glass supply stores, or glaziers for ideas. Long, pencil-like lampworking rods can be slid into clean PVC piping or cut to size and stacked in shallow plastic bins, all labeled with their COE and perhaps the manufacturer's name. Frit (ground glass) can be stored in zip-top bags, baby-food jars, spice containers, and so on. Each frit should be marked with its COE and its color or mix name, and marked as transparent or opaque. Store all your glass out of your studio's traffic flow but where it's conveniently within reach.

Lampworkers often use ground glass, called frit, when making beads. In this studio, the artist has stored frit in recycled baby food jars. The size is convenient, they have tight lids, and it's easy to identify frit colors when selecting glass for a project.

STORING TOOLS AND SUPPLIES

There are an extraordinary amount of things that you'll want to have in and around your studio. Finding the right place to put it all can be a daunting task; you'll notice that my recommendations won't send you to your local art glass supply center.

- **Storage benches:** Home improvement and garden furniture stores often sell kits for large storage benches (Keter is a popular brand, and its kits are easy to assemble). A storage bench or two in a studio provides seating for visitors, a place for large and oddly shaped items such as empty wine and beer bottles for lampworking, boxes of mosaic materials, lamp bases, fusing molds, and rolls of bubble wrap. Plastic storage benches are not an elegant solution, but they fulfill many studio needs very well.

- **Shelves:** Rather than wide, shallow shelves look for shelving units that are divided into nine to sixteen cells of equal size. The cells lock into each other, adding to the unit's stability. Because the cells are fairly narrow, they're stronger and less likely to sag when supporting heavy materials. Shelves are great for storing art books and supplies. The top can display standing items such as stained glass lamps, fused plates, and mosaics. If you want to store

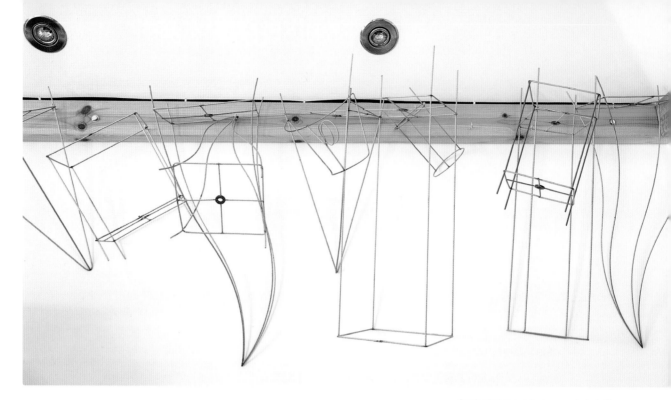

Create storage and display space by installing a wooden beam near the ceiling where you can hang tools, finished projects, and supplies.

glass here, move the unit a bit away from the wall to add depth for the glass sheets, and store the glass only on the bottom two shelves. Stand the sheets up on end; if you find that some glass sheets are too tall to fit, either cut them down to fit or store them near but not in the shelving unit.

- **Up, up, up:** In my last studio, my ceiling was covered with strong metal netting; I stored finished pieces by hanging them from the netting in an impromptu display. In my current studio, we installed wooden beams all around the room, where the wall meets the ceiling. I screwed in U-hooks where I display suncatchers and panels, and hang metal frames, rulers, and extra copper wires.

- **Tool chests with wheels:** These can be purchased from home improvement and hardware stores. They're excellent for storing finished pieces, materials for teaching assignments, and so on. Some tool chests are the right size and shape to serve as seats and can conveniently double as fair furniture after you unload your inventory. Others can be stacked, which saves space.

- **Kitchen and bathroom items:** Many items from kitchens and bathrooms make wonderful tool holders and storage bins in the glass art studio. Popsicle makers make excellent rod and tool caddies for lampworkers. Old-fashioned glass cookie jars make great reach-in-and-grab-it storage bins for little bags of frit and jewelry findings. Decorative wire shelving creates extra corner storage. Note, however, that what goes into your studio should not return to your kitchen or bathroom.

STORING CHEMICALS

Glass artists use a lot of chemicals—glues, patinas and flux, oils, glazes, etching creams, and more. Store chemicals in a dedicated cabinet out of the reach of children and pets, or put a lock on the cabinet door. Oils should be stored far from any lampworking torch, because oil will quickly corrode the tubing carrying the gas. This is a potentially explosive situation that can easily be prevented.

Placing your work in resealable bags is a convenient way to keep your items clean and neat while in storage. Keep several sizes of bags on hand for the different sizes of work that you create.

STORING FINISHED WORK

Finished work, if not displayed in the studio, should be carefully stored. Wrap your finished work in bubble wrap to lower the risk of breakage and to protect it from natural humidity and dust. Suncatchers with dangling wires can be closed in zip-top bags to prevent their wires from tangling, and then laid flat between layers of bubble wrap. Wrap panels in bubble wrap and store them standing on their side, like glass sheets. (If you can't visually identify the panel after it's wrapped, write a note on the outside with a permanent marker so that you won't have to unwrap everything when you are looking for a particular piece.) Plastic bins with drawers are convenient for small items such as jewelry. If you're setting aside fair inventory, store it in a toolbox and you'll be packed and ready for your next event.

Studio Safety

With a bit of thought and common sense, it's easy to identify many of the risks we face while working with glass. It's your responsibility as a glass worker to learn as much as possible and to take all necessary precautions to protect your health and well-being, and that of your studio visitors.

The following list does not include infrastructure issues (e.g., proper electrical installations, torch hardware, etc.), but information on these subjects can be found later in part 1 of the book. This outline is meant to guide you—but you are responsible for following safe work practices and ensuring that your studio is set up properly. If you're in doubt about a specific issue, consult with a local expert who can visit your studio and advise you. Never do anything that appears to be unsafe—love of glass is no justification for putting yourself at risk!

GENERAL RECOMMENDATIONS

- NEVER eat, drink, or smoke in your studio.
- Wear a heavy cotton or leather apron over your clothes, and wear closed shoes while you work.
- Tie back long hair.
- Have a good first-aid kit and water within reach.
- Keep your studio neat.

The author makes a lampworking safety fashion statement in longish sleeves, a heavy apron over natural-fiber clothing, and special safety glasses for flameworking. Her table has been cleared of combustibles, and she works over a fireproof marble slab. A fire extinguisher is on the floor, easily within reach.

- Wipe down surfaces with a damp cloth at the end of each project.
- Pick up stray pieces of glass and other materials, and then damp-mop your studio floor at the end of the day.
- Store all chemicals and glass powders out of the reach of children.
- Don't try to work when small children are around.
- Install great ventilation.

AVOIDING CUTS

- Take care when handling and grinding glass— it's easier to cut yourself than you'd expect, particularly when you're new to the craft.
- If your fingers slip and you drop a sheet of glass, resist the temptation to grab for it. Grabbing a large piece of falling glass is unsafe because you can slice open your palms and fingers. Do turn your face away to protect it from any flying shards.
- Break glass away from you, not toward you.
- Store your glass away from foot traffic.
- During projects, place the sheet and cut glass you're working with on flat surfaces, preferably in the center of your table. No piece should stick out over the edge of a surface where someone might run into it or accidentally put weight on it and flip it off the table.

SPECIAL PROTECTION

- Wear industrial safety glasses when cutting and grinding glass.
- Always ensure an adequate water level in the grinder basin before grinding glass.
- Wear protective clothing and special lampworking glasses when working with a torch. If you frequently work with glass that "spits" as it heats in the flame, consider wearing a didymium face shield instead of glasses, and long sleeves.
- Visitors observing torch work should wear protective glasses and stand clear of the flame.

- Wear a respiratory mask when preparing glazes, bead separator, or kiln wash from powder when working with frit or powdered glass and when cleaning a fusing kiln after a firing.
- Use a tabletop fume collector or mobile hood when soldering.

AVOIDING BURNS AND FIRE HAZARDS

- Make your studio as fireproof as possible by removing combustibles and adding heat-proof surfaces.
- While lampworking, always rest the hot end of glass rods away from you, on a metal rod rest.
- Remember: Glass, metal, and tools used to solder or melt glass will stay hot for a long time, even if they appear cool.
- Keep a working fire extinguisher in your studio and know how to use it.
- When soldering edges of a piece, don't hold the soldering iron over your hands—grasp the glass from the side to avoid burns from solder drips.
- Be mindful of the soldering iron when it's hot— always rest it on its stand when not in use. Never reach to pick up the soldering iron unless you're looking at it. Verify that it's not touching anything combustible, such as a piece of pattern paper, when it's resting.
- Wait to open your kiln until it has returned to room temperature, and disconnect the electrical power to your fusing kiln before opening the lid. Empty the kiln only after the glass has cooled.

CHEMICAL SAFETY

- Don't store or use oils near your torch station.
- Wear latex gloves when applying patinas or working with grout. If your skin is sensitive, wear gloves while applying flux, too.
- Cover all cuts and scratches with a bandage to prevent contamination from chemicals or lead.
- At the end of each studio session, and before you eat or drink, wash your hands with an industrial soap that removes heavy metal residues.

Clockwise from upper left: a disposable respiratory mask, industrial safety glasses, D-Lead soap, aloe vera gel, bandages, a disposable latex glove, and lampworking safety glasses

More about Ventilation

Why is ventilation so important? Art glass is colored with a variety of minerals and metals, many of which are released into the air as glass heats. When we solder, we melt a mix of lead and tin and create a toxic lead vapor. (Hot flux fumes aren't so good for us, either.) Fine fibers and finely ground powers, including glass, can become airborne. Glues, paints, and certain cleaners contain solvents that evaporate and mix into the air. All these can be inhaled, and in some cases, absorbed by soft tissues such as our eyes. Some settle in our lungs, where they might eventually cause silicosis, while others dissolve into our bloodstream and travel to other parts of our body.

This isn't to say that glass working is horribly dangerous—these are risks that glass workers have managed and overcome with safe working practices for thousands of years.

Glass Studio
Tools and Supplies

Kilns

Any type of studio work that relies on heating glass demands a kiln. For many glass artists, it's the most expensive equipment we'll ever buy, so it's worth putting some thought into which kiln will best meet your needs.

Fused Art Mosaic tile by Mette Enøe

DIFFERENT KILN TYPES

All kilns should have controlled heating and cooling capabilities, monitored by a digital controller. Lampworking kilns, fusing kilns, and ceramic kilns are similar but different types of equipment and are not interchangeable.

Lampworking kilns are usually small, table-top kilns with windows or doors that open on the side of the kiln. They are used for annealing small objects such as handmade glass beads and sculptures to guarantee the structural integrity of the glass after you have worked with it.

Fusing kilns are usually heavier floor units and come in many sizes. While your choice of kiln will undoubtedly be influenced by cost, consider the ways you intend to use it and how much space you have in your studio. If you'll only be fusing jewelry, a smaller fusing kiln will

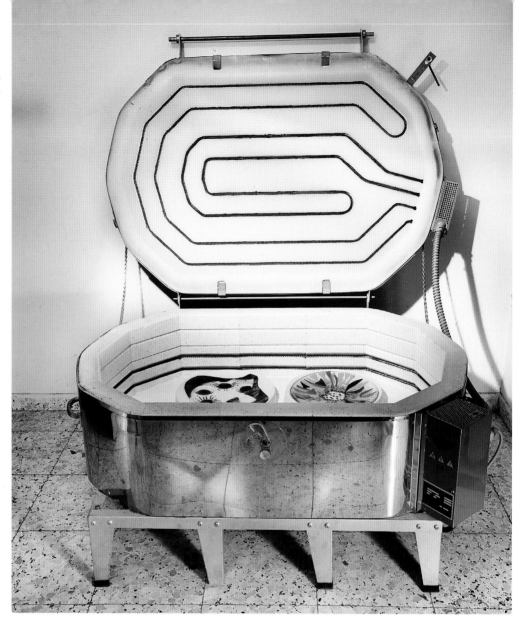

A full-sized fusing kiln, with heating spirals in the lid.

be adequate. If you plan on creating large platters or elements for stained glass masterpieces, or hope to teach fusing in a workshop or classroom setting, invest in a bigger fusing kiln.

Note that there are exceptions: It's sometimes possible to fuse very small items in a lampworking kiln (verify in the kiln's specifications), and fusing kilns can be used to *batch-anneal* beads. Batch-anneal means that instead of placing the beads in a kiln as you make them, you first cool them without a kiln, then kiln-anneal them at a later time. (Batch annealing is covered in more detail in part 2, chapter 5, "Lampworking.")

Ceramic kilns, in general, are not appropriate for glass work because of their heating design and overall shape. Ceramic kilns are usually smaller in diameter but taller than fusing kilns. Intense heat is generated from coils in the sides of the kiln (rather than in the lid, as in glass fusing kilns). The pottery in the kiln is stacked on shelves, and the heat in the kiln varies by the height of the open space and how many items are stacked inside. In glass work, this variation of heat is undesirable. A glass fusing kiln is usually only tall enough for one layer of glass work but is much wider, to accommodate large items and a fair quantity of items in each fusing.

ELECTRICAL CONSIDERATIONS

A less recognized but very important consideration is the kiln's requirements for electrical power. While some small kilns can operate on regular household current, most fusing kilns require a heavier current and a special electrical socket. Installing this modification is a job for a certified electrician. Not every home or studio has access to heavy current, nor will every fuse box support heavy electrical use. Verify the electrical requirements for the kiln you're considering and consult with an electrician *before* you make a purchase. Also, verify whether the kiln you're considering is set up for the standard current in your country of residence. Many manufacturers offer different versions, so read the small print carefully before buying, particularly if you're ordering equipment from a website.

Large fusing kilns often require special electrical installations.

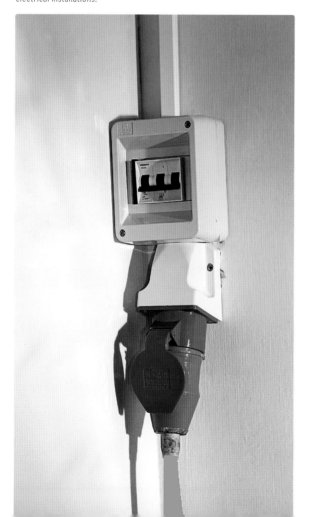

Safety Alert!

A critical difference between fusing kilns and lampworking kilns is that electrical heating coils are set into open channels in the insides and lid of the fusing kiln, where you might accidentally touch them.

WHEN FUSING

The exposed coils in a fusing kiln don't pose a danger to us because we load fusing kilns before we turn them on, don't (as a rule) open the kiln while it's in operation, and unload the kiln after the firing is finished and the kiln has cooled. As a safety precaution, always disconnect the electrical supply before opening a fusing kiln after a firing.

WHILE LAMPWORKING

While lampworking, we must open the door of the kiln while it's running; immediately after making each bead, we place the bead into a hot kiln. Lampwork beads are formed on metal sticks called *mandrels*; as a safety measure, the heating elements of proper lampworking kilns are hidden inside the kiln's walls and floor to prevent us from potentially touching the electrical elements with a mandrel and shocking or burning ourselves.

A lampworking kiln, filled with beads on mandrels

THE ART OF HEATING AND COOLING GLASS

Glass can't be heated suddenly without breaking. When we raise the temperature in our kiln from room temperature to our target temperature at a slow, steady rate, the glass can adjust to the new temperatures. When lampworking, we must heat the glass gradually in the flame before fully melting it. Likewise, cooling glass to room temperature must happen at a controlled rate in a controlled environment—a kiln—or the glass might crack.

Lampworking and fusing processes introduce physical stress that can fatally weaken the structure of your piece. The stress can be released, strengthening your piece, with a process called *annealing*. Each type of glass is structurally and chemically unique; each tolerates a specific rate of temperature change, each melts at a different temperature, and each requires resting at specific temperature points for specific periods. It might seem that you need a degree in physics before you fire up a kiln, but it's not as complicated as it sounds. For almost every process and type of glass, there's a firing schedule. We program the firing schedule into a digital controller that, together with the kiln's pyrometer, continually monitors and regulates the temperature inside the kiln. To download the author's firing and annealing schedules visit www.glassandlight.blogspot.com. You can also go to Quarry's website at www.quarrybooks.com and search for *The Glass Artist's Studio Handbook* and find a link to them there.

The larger beads were annealed in a kiln. The smaller beads were flame-annealed and cooled between two pieces of fiber blanket. The smaller beads broke shortly after being removed from their mandrels.

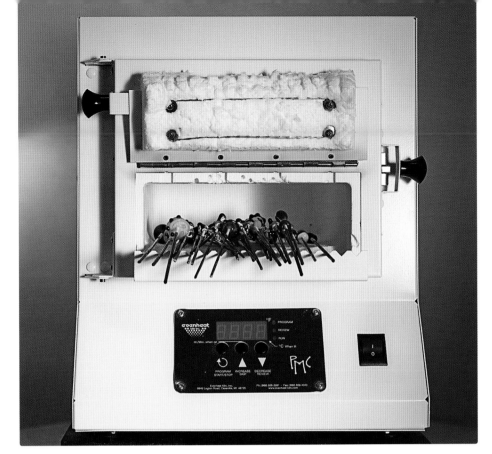

The built-in controller of this lamp-working kiln is programmed with the tree black buttons seen below the open kiln door. The red display in the center of the panel will show the kiln temperature when the kiln is turned on. The kiln's on-off switch is to the right of the controller's panel.

THE IMPORTANCE OF KILN ANNEALING

Beginning lampworkers often balk at purchasing a kiln, either foregoing annealing altogether or relying on an alternative process referred to as *flame annealing*. If you consider the points from the previous section, particularly that each piece of glass must rest (or soak) at specific temperatures for a specific number of minutes in order to release stress and bond with structural strength, it's easy to understand why I don't recommend bypassing the annealing process or substituting flame annealing.

Pieces that aren't properly annealed might break as they cool, or they might break months later when they're subjected to a slight shock, such as a door slamming nearby or being placed roughly on a table. Although it's not visually apparent, the structural integrity of an unannealed piece is uncertain. Its future, though, is unfortunately predictable. A lampworking acquaintance who flame-anneals told me that at least 30 percent of her beads break before she ever strings them on a necklace.

Digital Controllers

Digital controllers are electronic instruments coupled to your kiln that turn the heating coils on and off to control the temperature and speed of temperature change. They're calibrated to give precise results. A quick glance at a controller display will inform you of how long the kiln has been running, what the temperature is inside the kiln, and what stage of the firing process is running. Even if you purchased a used kiln, consider purchasing a new digital controller.

Each digital controller is programmed a little differently, and manufacturers generally provide instructions for turning on the controller, entering data, and starting the firing process. Firing schedules are programmed into a controller by the user in *steps*. Each step includes the **Rate** of temperature change, **Target** temperature, and **Hold** time (expressed in the following example as hours.minutes). A schedule can have many steps, defined by the glass and process you're working with.

How to Read a Kiln Firing Schedule and Program Your Controller

It's crucial to note that there are two definitions of **Rate**: In my schedules, I name them differently (Rd vs. Rm), but in most books and controller instructions, they're simply named R and the user must do the calculations. Read the manufacturer's instructions for your controller and know which Rate your controller uses! The steps used in the following examples are identical, as are the final results, although the Rate is calculated and programmed differently.

In the first type of controller, Rate refers to how many *degrees* the kiln temperature must change in one hour (R*d*). If Step 1 is to gradually raise the temperature of the kiln to 500 degrees over two hours, and to hold the kiln at 500 degrees for ten minutes, Rd would refer to the number of *degrees* the temperature should rise *each hour* and the step would be programmed as:

ST1: Rd250 – T500 – H0.10

In the second type of controller, Rate refers to how many *minutes* will be spent to reach the target temperature (R*m*). If Step 1 is to gradually raise the temperature of the kiln to 500 degrees over two hours, and to hold the kiln at 500 degrees for ten minutes, Rm would refer to the number of *minutes* spent reaching the target temperature and the step would be programmed as:

ST1: Rm120 – T500 – H0.10

In addition, some digital controllers require that time be entered as minutes only. For a controller that recognizes Hold only in minutes, you must convert the Hold listed in the author's fusing schedules to a new value. H2.10 (two hours and ten minutes), for example, would equal H130 (130 minutes).

USEFUL TERMS:

When you program a kiln rate as **FULL,** you're instructing the kiln to change temperature as quickly as possible. To **SKIP** is to deliberately move on to the next step of a kiln firing before the previous step has finished. **STOP**, or **END**, instructs the digital controller to end the firing. Read your controller instructions to learn how to carry out Full, Skip, and Stop for your kiln.

Program your controller and start your lampworking kiln *before* lighting your torch. Turn on and program your controller *after* loading your fusing kiln and shutting the lid. Some controllers have preprogrammed firing schedules or allow you to save a program once you've used it. But even if you save a program into your controller, you should keep a fusing diary.

An external controller for large fusing kilns

A fully loaded kiln, after firing

Keeping a Fusing Diary

Every kiln has its quirks—some fire better on the sides, some in the center. Not all pyrometers measure temperature identically, due to slight differences in calibration and the shape of the kiln. Your pyrometer, however, should read a specific temperature point in the same way each time you fire the kiln. To get the best performance from your kiln, keep a fusing diary to note what works and what doesn't.

1. Set aside a notebook as a dedicated fusing diary; use one page per firing.

2. At the top of the page, write what task you're performing and the COE for this firing—Full Fuse Spectrum, Slump COE 90, and so forth.

3. In the first paragraph, write your fusing schedule, step by step.

4. In the second paragraph, note the type of glass, the number of layers, the average size of the fused pieces, if the kiln was full, half full, one-quarter full, and so on. Note where you placed the items—in the center, at the right side, and so forth. If you've included glazed items, note their colors and their location in the kiln.

5. After firing, examine the pieces before removing them from the kiln. Enter your opinion of the fuse—for instance, poor, excellent, best in the center—and note any highlights or problems.

6. If, after examining the firing results, you decide that this is a schedule you'll want to use again, mark it with a big, easy-to-see notation such as a star.

Keep the diary within easy reach of the kiln and refer to it before every firing. If you write down all your successes and failures and adjust your firing schedules accordingly, your work can improve with every firing.

Your bead annealing schedules should be noted in your diary, too. If you have more than one kiln, add a notation at the top of each page clearly indicating which kiln you're using.

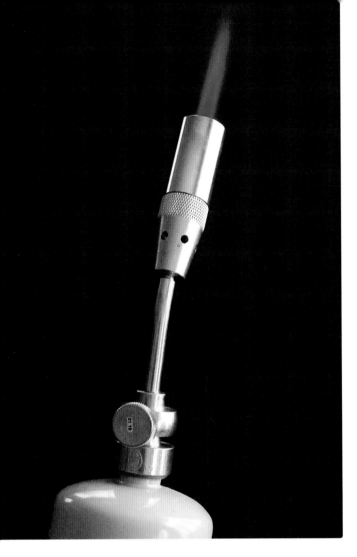

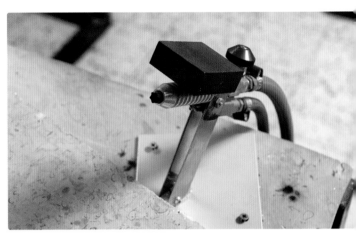

Lampworking Torches

A lampworking torch produces a sword-like flame that's hot enough to melt glass. Most run on a combination of gas and oxygen that's piped into the torch through rubber hoses manufactured for use with pressurized gas.

SELECTING A TORCH

The Hot Head Bead Torch

The **Hot Head** is a simple, low-tech torch, perhaps the least expensive way to start beadmaking. It doesn't require extensive hardware as do many other setups. You manually screw the torch head into a fuel canister and open the gas flow with a small knob before lighting the flame. The torch head sucks in air during operation, which feeds the gas flame but is noisy. If replacement gas canisters aren't available in your location, adapters can be purchased to connect the Hot Head to larger gas tanks.

The Hot Head is appropriate for working with soft glass; it's a good beginner's torch for crafters who are exploring lampworking for the first time, people whose funds are limited, and beadmakers who prefer low-tech, portable tools. While some professionals prefer this torch, many eventually upgrade to a bench burner.

Small Bench Burners

The next step up in complexity and strength is a small bench burner. All the lampworking projects in this book were made with a small bench burner. Bench burners are clamped or screwed onto the top of the workstation and are fueled by a steady supply of oxygen and gas. The user has control over the ratio of gas to oxygen, which is useful for bringing out colors and shine on silvered glasses. Smaller bench burners have a fairly narrow flame and aren't recommended for very large projects.

Large Bench Burners

Larger bench burners tend to be named after aggressive animals such as barracudas; their hotter, larger flame is often fueled by more than one gas hose and more than one oxygen hose.

ASSOCIATED HARDWARE

You will need the following hardware to work with your torch:

Gas tanks: Torches require a continuous gas supply. Some lampworkers use specialty gasses for this. Consult with your local gas suppliers to understand what your options are. Gas can be supplied by cylinder, tank, pipeline, and canister.

Oxygen tanks: Bench burners require a supply of oxygen, which can be purchased in cylinders and delivered to your door. They must be coupled to the torch with hoses, like the gas tanks. Both types of tanks should have regulators and backflow arrestors installed. Gas and oxygen tanks should be stored outdoors, and the laws in your location may require additional infrastructure such as chains or other physical containment.

O_2 concentrators: Concentrators are machines designed for the medical world; they pull in air from the room, clean it, and expel it as pure oxygen. Lampworking doesn't require the high purity used in hospitals, so most lampworkers who use concentrators purchase used, refurbished machines. O_2 concentrators are linked to bench burners with rubber hosing, but they don't require regulators. They require electricity to operate, and their filters must be replaced periodically.

Regulators: Most lampworkers install regulators on their gas and oxygen tanks to control the flow to their torches. Oxygen regulators and gas regulators aren't identical—read the package carefully before purchasing.

Hoses/tubing: High-pressure compressed gas and oxygen flow through special hoses made especially for this. The hose is clamped to the gas supply on one end and to the torch on the other. The seal must be airtight. When checking for potential leaks, use soapy water and look for bubbles. Never use oil, which quickly corrodes the hosing, leading to leaks and other dangers.

TIP | **Buying Hardware**

In theory, it should be possible to purchase and learn everything you need from your local glass art supply house. In practice, though, many of us live far from such services. Torches and equipment can be purchased over the Internet, or you can look in a store or supply center for people who do renovations or construction. In my experience, they not only sell the equipment, but also understand very well how to use it. I recommend you consult with a local expert who knows the equipment available in your area and who will be able to help you make informed decisions.

Backflow arrestors: Although it's rare, the torch flame can flow back into the hoses until it reaches the supply tank, causing fire and explosions. Prevent this by installing backflow arrestors.

Clamps and vises: For your safety and the safety of those around you, you must either clamp or screw the torch to the table firmly. Some people prefer to use a U vise to clamp the workstation, but screwing the base plate into the tabletop is the safest method.

Fire extinguisher: Have a working fire extinguisher within reach. Check its gauge periodically to verify that it's still pressurized, and read the instructions to refresh your memory on how to use it.

SETTING UP A TORCH STATION

- Your torch station will start with a table. If the surface isn't fireproof, you must add something to make it so; a metal sheet, ceramic tiles, or a slab of marble will do the job.

On this torch, the gas knob (at top) is red and the oxygen knob (not visible) is silver. The hoses for gas and oxygen are also made from different colors.

Safety Alert!

Don't leave your gas hoses full. After extinguishing the torch, close all gas and oxygen sources (not just the knobs on the torch). Once you're sure there's no gas or oxygen flowing into the hoses from the source tanks, open the knobs on the torch and release all residual gas and oxygen from the hoses. This is called bleeding—the amount released is very small but will give your hoses longer life.

A backflow arrestor

- If you're using an oxygen concentrator, place it under or near the table and plug it into the electricity. The back filters should be unobstructed.
- If you're using cylinders or tanks for oxygen and/ or gas, they should be outside. Have an expert install them.
- Have a quick-couple or emergency gas switch installed in your studio.
- Install regulators on your tanks—ask your gas supplier or local experienced lampworker to help you.
- Prepare lengths of rubber hosing—buy the kind that's specifically manufactured for use with high-pressured gas. Common usage is red for gas and blue or green for oxygen. Install the backflow arrestors along the hosing, according to the instructions in the packet, before attaching the torch to the hoses. Be sure to read the torch manufacturer's instructions as to where to hook up the gas and where to hook up the oxygen.
- Attach the hoses to your in-room gas supply.
- Make sure the torch knobs are closed. Open each tank and adjust the regulator according to the manufacturer's (or expert's) instructions.
- Before lighting the torch for the first time, open the oxygen supply to the torch. Use soapy water to check for leaks along all the lines and connections from the source tank to the torch. If there are leaks, you'll see bubbles (even very small bubbles indicate a leak!). Fix any leaks and check again. Once you're certain there are no leaks, close the oxygen supply. Open the gas supply and check for leaks. Once you're sure there are no leaks, close the gas supply.
- Place a working fire extinguisher in the room.

Hand Tools and Other Supplies

GLASS CUTTERS

Although the process is commonly called cutting glass, and the tools are usually called *glass cutters,* technically we don't cut glass—we scratch and break it. The scratching action is called *scoring,* and the breaking action is called *opening.* A variety of glass cutting tools are available and, with practice, it's possible to cut almost every shape out of glass. A detailed explanation and glass cutting exercises are provided in part 2, in the section "Cutting Glass." The following tools are used to score and open glass:

- **Tile nippers:** Tile nippers look like scissors but have carbide or steel disks instead of scissor blades. Some suppliers call them mosaic nippers or wheel cutters. It's hard to cut a precise shape using a tile nipper, which breaks glass without scoring it first. Hold the glass between the tile nipper's disks and squeeze the handles shut against the glass, increasing the pressure until the glass cracks into pieces. Squeezing the disks close to the edge of the glass will result in a curved break. Tile nippers can be used to cut art glass, lampworking rods, and mosaic tiles. This tool can be purchased from glass art supply stores and hardware stores.

- **Glass cutters:** These tools are used to score glass along the line where we'd like the glass to break. We then apply pressure under the score to break the glass. Simple glass cutters—a pencil-like stick with a metal wheel at one end and perhaps a metal ball at the other—can usually be found in hardware and craft stores. When not in use, glass cutters should be placed blade down in a cup or jar, resting on a felt pad or sponge soaked with cutting oil. With practice, it's possible to cut very precise shapes with a glass cutter. A simple glass cutter provides excellent service and isn't difficult to cut with, even if it doesn't have all the tempting swivel heads, built-in oil wells, special blades, and pistol grips of the more expensive models manufactured specifically for glass artists. In this book, the expression "cutting glass" means scoring with a glass

From left to right: Blue Runner, Ring Star, tile nipper, and glass cutter

cutter and opening the glass along the score line, or breaking glass with a tile nipper.

- **Glass saws** or **ring saws:** These electric saws are designed specifically to cut sheets of glass. They're large, expensive, and, according to one of our featured artists, loud and messy. While it's possible to make a very precise cut with a saw, including tight curves and angles that can't be cut by hand, I don't recommend them for beginners' studios, and I don't use one myself. After you've mastered the art of cutting with a glass cutter, you'll be better able to judge whether a glass saw is a tool that will truly be useful in your studio.

CUTTING AIDS

The following items will improve your cutting precision and safety:

- **Cutting oil** is a general name for oil that protects the blade of your glass cutter at rest, traps the small bits of glass released as you score glass, and deepens your scores, making them easier to open. Glass art supply shops sell cutting oil specifically for stained glass, but thin mechanical oils such as sewing machine oil work just as well.

- A **Blue Runner** is a type of **running pliers** and is a handy tool for breaking glass along a straight score; after scoring the glass, place the glass between the tool's jaws with the score running exactly down the center (toward your hand). Squeeze until the glass snaps in two along the score. The Blue Runner has a raised line on one side of the jaw—this should be on top, over the score.

- A **Ring Star** is another type of **running pliers** used to open curved scores. It's similar to a Blue Runner but with a rounded end; the lower jaw has a small raised cone. After scoring the glass, slide the glass between the jaws. Place the cone exactly under the score and squeeze once or twice, very gently. Move down the score's curve and squeeze again, exactly along the score. You might have to go over the entire score several times before the score opens and the glass breaks into two pieces. Using a Ring Star takes patience and practice but gives excellent results. Blue Runners and Ring Stars are specifically glass art tools and must be purchased from a glass art supply shop.

- **Pliers** are an all-purpose studio tool. As a glass cutting aid, pliers can grasp and snap off small pieces that didn't separate from a score, can be used to snap off strips (in lieu of a Blue Runner), and can be used to tap along the underside of a score to weaken it before opening it. Pliers can be purchased in a hardware store.

- A **cutting pad** is a soft cloth or piece of thin carpet that you lay over your workboard before cutting glass. It provides a slight cushion and a flat surface; without a pad, you could scratch or crack the underside of your glass as you score with the glass cutter. I use large rectangles of felt, sold in the cleaning supplies aisle of my local supermarket for wiping down countertops, and replace the pad when it gets very dirty or tears. Cutting pads must be shaken clean frequently as you work.

GENERAL TOOLS AND SUPPLIES

- **Workboards** are large, flat pieces of wood that are placed over a table to protect it and are used as a strong, flat work surface for cutting glass and soldering. They should be large enough to completely support projects and thick enough that they won't warp over time. The workboard surface should be smooth and unfinished, without paint or varnish. The workboard must be brushed clear of all dirt, glass bits, and solder drips before you lay down the cutting pad.

- **Permanent/waterproof markers** can be used to write on glass and to trace patterns. The ink will wash off with soap and water and will burn off in a hot kiln.

- **Pattern paper** can be used to make patterns for stained glass and fusing projects. Any kind of heavy paper can be used; buy cheap art paper at an office supply or craft store. Typing paper is too thin to make patterns with.

- **Pencils/pens/erasers/rulers/colored pencils** are all helpful for making patterns.

- **Metal snips** look like pliers with sharp jaws. Sometimes you can use your pliers as a metal snip, and some tools are made specifically for cutting metal.

TIP | **What Else?**

Other items that you'll need in your studio include safety glasses, cotton balls, latex gloves, paper towels, dishwashing liquid, an old toothbrush, ribbon, string or wire for hanging your creations, jewelry pliers, and findings such as chains, crimp beads, and earring hooks.

GRINDING AIDS

- **Grinding stones,** also called abrasive stones, come in several sizes and materials. Hold the stone in your hand and rub the edges of the cut glass with the side of the stone in a circular motion, under water. Grinding stones are a sensible choice when you're new to glass craft because they're cheap. When you feel confident that you'll continue working with glass, buy a glass grinder; working with a grinding stone is tedious, and an electric grinder does a far better job.

- **Glass grinders** are electric tools with a small engine enclosed in waterproof housing, a pool or reservoir for water, a grinding head (which can be replaced with a drill bit when needed), and a perforated work surface. Generally there's a sponge to wick water from the reservoir to the drill head. The simplest electric grinders are sufficient for even a professional studio, as long as the grinder heads can be replaced when they wear down.

Using pattern shears

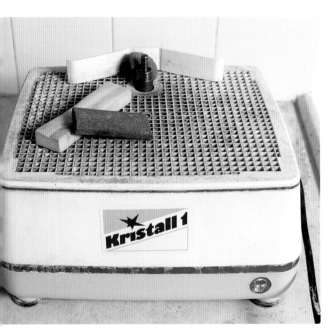

Grinding stones resting on an electric grinder

TOOLS AND SUPPLIES: STAINED GLASS

- **Copper foil** is indispensable in the stained glass studio. It comes in rolls of thin strips backed with glue and paper. It can be purchased from glass art supply shops and some craft stores. The projects in this book should be made with standard ¼" or $^7/_{32}$"-width foil unless stated otherwise.

- **Pattern shears** are double-bladed scissors. As you cut out a paper pattern, the shears remove a small channel of paper between the pattern pieces that the copper foil will eventually fill. Pattern shears are marked either for lead work or for copper foil work. (Lead requires a wider channel than copper foil.)

- **Burnishers** are, generally speaking, straight plastic sticks with smooth edges.

- **Soldering irons** are electric tools manufactured for a variety of work. The irons made for electronics work aren't hot enough for stained glass work; purchase a stained glass soldering iron from a glass art supply shop. If budget allows, buy a strong iron

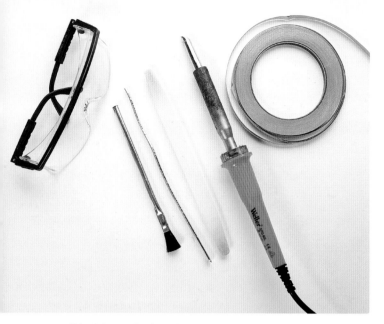

Stained glass supplies, from left to right: industrial safety glasses, a flux brush, a stick of solder, a burnisher, a soldering iron, and a roll of copper foil

with a built-in thermostat. Soldering irons usually come with stands. You'll need to buy **soldering flux** (a fluid or paste that preps the copper foil for soldering) and a **flux brush** to apply the flux.

- Stained glass **solder** is available in a standard lead and tin mix or in a lead-free mix of tin and silver or pewter. It can be purchased as sticks or spools. Solder for electronics shouldn't be used as it contains chemical additives.

- **Soldering rags** are used to clean the tip of the soldering iron as you work. They should be 100 percent cotton or they'll melt and stick to the tip of the iron. Recycle old socks or tear up an old t-shirt to make soldering rags. Before each soldering session, dampen the cloth with clean water, wring it out, and fold it into a pad about the size of a deck of playing cards. Place it on the top corner of the workboard where you can reach it easily with the soldering iron. If the rag gets warm or dirty during a long work session, refold it to expose a cleaner side or rinse it with cool water.

- **Lead came** and **lead ribbons** are molded from pure lead and are used in traditional stained glass construction to create a metal belt around glass

pieces. The came is named by the letter it looks like: *H* came, for example, is open on both sides and is used in the center of panels to form a border between adjacent pieces of glass that are fitted into the open top and bottom of the *H*. In copper foil construction, *U* came is used to create smooth, protective borders around the outside of panels. Lead ribbons are thin and long. They can be formed into hanging loops or decorative lead squiggles and curls.

- **Wire** and **beads** can be used to decorate stained glass pieces and to create hanging loops. Uncoated steel wire is available in hardware stores and garden centers. Brass and copper wire can also be used. Colorful nylon-wrapped jewelry wire is a strong and attractive material to use for hanging suncatchers.

- Stained glass supply shops sell **patina**, a mild acid used to color metal solder seams.

- **Finishing compounds for stained glass** such as oil or wax must be applied to stained glass seams to prevent them from corroding and weakening your piece.

Examples of lead ribbon and came

Safety Alert!

Lead is a solid metal and isn't hazardous in stained glass windows or suncatchers. However, lead-free solder should always be used when making stained glass jewelry because leaded solder shouldn't be worn on the skin. Likewise, don't use stained glass techniques to create dishes, canisters, or cups that might come in direct contact with food or drink, even if you use lead-free solder.

TOOLS AND SUPPLIES: FUSING

- **Slumping molds** can be made from carved fire brick, heat-resistant metal, fiberboard, and plaster.
- **Kiln wash** is a thin ceramic compound that protects the kiln floor and molds during a firing; hot glass can't bond to surfaces that have been coated with kiln wash.
- **Kiln wash brushes** are wide and very soft so as not to leave marks in the kiln wash that you brush onto the mold or the kiln bottom.
- **Glass glue**, also known as fusing glue and tack-glue, is manufactured especially for fusing work. This mild adhesive will help hold pieces in place before you put them in a kiln for firing. Fusing glue burns cleanly in the kiln, without leaving any residue or discoloring the glass.
- **Glass glazes** are specialty paints that are fused into the surface of glass.
- **Fiber papers** are resistant to heat. The thinnest fiber paper, also called **kiln shelf paper**, is used to protect the floor of the kiln during a fusing session.

TOOLS AND SUPPLIES: LAMPWORKING

- **Mandrels** are thin steel rods used as a base for beads. They can be purchased from lampworking suppliers. Some construction supply stores sell very long rods and will cut them for you, but you must file down the ends before use. Mandrels come in many sizes.
- **Bead separator** is a liquid ceramic compound. Mandrels are dipped in bead separator before they're used. Buy premade bead separator or powder from a glass art supply shop.
- **Marvers** are graphite, stone, or metal blocks that hot glass can be pressed against. Some are textured or have handles. Some people make their own marvers, but it's easiest to buy one.
- **Mashers** are tools with long handles and flat or textured pieces on the end. Squeeze hot glass between masher blades to change the glass's shape.
- **Hemostats** are medical tools adopted by glass artists. With long handles that can be locked, and fancy jaws with ridges or teeth, they're convenient for holding bits of glass near the flame.

Fusing supplies, clockwise from bottom: fiberboard, stainless steel bowl, kiln shelf paper, plaster mold, and kiln wash brush

- **Rod rests** are metal stands, usually with ridges on top, for resting hot glass and tools during a lampworking session.
- **Presses** are like carved double-sided marvers; lay the mandrel and hot glass between the top and bottom parts and press the hot glass into shape.
- **Picks** can be tungsten picks, dental picks, or other metal picks. They're used to rake designs in hot glass and to poke depressions in the surface of hot beads.
- **BBQ lighters** are like large cigarette lighters with long metal ends. They're very convenient for lighting torches safely.
- **Glass shears** are used to slice hot glass. A simple and inexpensive type of glass shears preferred by many lampworkers are actually tomato shears (used in agriculture) from China.
- **Scalpels** are used to cut glass, move, and shape it.
- **Tweezers** are used to pull glass strings, remove unwanted bits, and flatten edges of bits of glass to make shapes such as fish fins and petals.
- **Vermiculite/fiber blanket** can be used to cool lampwork beads if you don't have a lampworking kiln. Neither option anneals your beads. If you intend to use vermiculite, you must fill a large, fireproof container. The vermiculite must be deep enough that you can plunge hot beads into it. To lessen the percentage of beads that break when cooled in vermiculite, place the vermiculate in a ceramic crock pot (electric slow-cooker) and heat

the vermiculite before starting your lampworking session. Keep the pot hot until the end of the lampworking session, and lower the temperature gradually over a few hours. Let the beads cool in the vermiculite until morning. This is a good solution if you plan to batch anneal later.

The Simple Start-Up Studio

When you're just starting out, you might not have a lot of room, many tools, or a big glass inventory; with time, you'll understand that most glass artists never feel they have enough room, tools, or glass. Still, there's a minimum you should strive for.

SAFETY FIRST

Never take shortcuts on safety; you'll need safety glasses, latex gloves, bandages, burn cream, a fire extinguisher (except for mosaics), lampworking glasses (lampworking only), disposable respiratory masks, and a work apron.

Safety Alert!

Contrary to what you occasionally read on websites or in books, sunglasses (of any kind) cannot substitute for lampworking safety glasses. Always wear proper lampworking safety glasses when working with a torch, to protect your sight.

FURNITURE AND WORKSTATIONS

- A **worktable:** If your chosen technique is stained glass or mosaics, this should be a large table. If you're making beads, fireproof the surface and clamp the torch to the table's edge where the flame will point in a safe direction.
- A **sink** and **counter space:** These will come in handy for washing your work, and accommodating a glass grinder and a basin of water.
- **Lighting** and **ventilation:** You'll want some of both.
- **Storage solutions:** If you're very short on space, use a storage bench on wheels; you can fill it with tools, materials, or finished art, sit on it as you work, and roll it under your table when you're not working. If you're working in a spare bedroom, shallow storage bins can be stashed under the bed.

HAND TOOLS AND MATERIALS

- **For stained glass:** a glass cutter, a tile nipper, a cutting pad, a jar with cutting oil, pliers, a grinding stone, copper foil, a burnisher, a soldering iron, flux, solder, and finishing compound.
- **For fusing:** a kiln, a glass cutter, shelf paper, kiln wash, and a kiln wash brush. If you want to make fused jewelry, but you don't have the room (or the budget) for a full-sized fusing kiln, try a small microwave kiln. (As the name suggests, they fit in your microwave.) While they can't fuse large projects, they're relatively cheap.
- **For lampworking:** a torch (and all associated hardware and gas/oxygen supply), mandrels, a marver, bead release, a small tabletop kiln such as a Chili Pepper Bead Annealer, a fiber blanket, or a crock pot for vermiculite.

Table of Layout Needs by Technique, for One Person

	Stained Glass	Fusing	Lampworking
Wet workstation	X	X	X
Drying station	X	X	X
Glass cutting & prep workstation	Note: Table must be cleaned well between techniques.		
Soldering station	X*		
Torch station			X
Glass storage	X	>1	>1
Chemical storage	X	X	
Kiln		X	X
Storage	A lot	A little	A lot
Glass art display	The more visitors you expect, the more display you'll want.		
Visitor seating	If you open your studio to visitors on a regular basis		
Refreshment corner	Depending on your business model		
Bathroom	Particularly if you teach or welcome visitors		

* Note: Table must be cleaned well between processes.

Exploring Glass:
Basic Techniques

Selecting Glass

Few of us manufacture our own glass; fortunately, art glass is readily available in many forms—sheets, rods, canes, and frit—as well as in a rainbow of colors and textures.

You're probably most familiar with common sheet glass, also called *float*. This is the type of glass used to make windows—it's flat, smooth, and colorless. Not all sheet glass is the same. Art glass is available in many colors, and the manufacturing process can add air bubbles, ribbons of different colors, and textures. Some patterned glass seems to have a visual direction of flow, which you can take advantage of in your design. Transparency versus opacity will shift when a sheet of glass is held up to the light. Some brands of glass are easier to cut than others, and there's a huge variation in price that fluctuates by manufacturer, the intended use of the glass, and the glass color. Red, for instance, is made with genuine gold, and all the colors in the red-purple spectrum are usually more expensive than glass in the blue-green spectrum.

When you purchase glass as a mosaic or stained glass artist, you'll need to consider all these factors. If you already have a project in mind, bring your pattern to the store with you to pick out glass. Sheet glass sold for cold work (mosaics, stained glass) is usually sold by size and makes no mention of the physical properties of the glass, because you don't need that information to work with it.

COE: THE HIDDEN PROPERTY OF GLASS

Fusers also work with sheet glass, but with a twist: They must consider the physical properties of the glass they choose. Fusing glass and lampworking rods are identified by **COE**, short for **coefficiency of expansion**. When glass heats, it expands; when it cools, it contracts, but not to exactly the same size as it started, and the difference is expressed as COE. What's most important for you to know is that all the glass used in a specific project must be of the same COE family. In a reliable glass supply store, art glass for warm and hot work will be stored by COE family in separate locations, clearly labeled, to avoid mixing them. You should do the same in your studio because

---

Ready-to-use art glass components are sold in home décor stores as filler for vases and in craft supply shops. They're available in many colors, sizes, and glass types, but because we can't guess their physical properties, they can't be used in warm or hot work. They are, however, a splendid addition to mosaics and stained glass.

Nuggets are round and flat, like melted marbles. *Jewels* are glass copies of gemstone cuts. *Crystals* are 3-D faceted shapes that throw shards of light when direct sunlight shines through them. *Squiggles* are curved and flat on one side and difficult to apply copper foil to. *Prisms* and *bevels* have angled edges that reflect rainbows. *Molded cabs* might look like leaves, the sun, a face, or even a killer whale!

it's impossible to identify COE by the way a piece of glass looks. Keeping your COE families separate is critical for the future integrity of your projects. You can write the COE number on a piece of glass with a waterproof felt pen; the ink will wash off with dishwashing liquid and water, or burn off when fired in a kiln.

Other common forms of glass are rods (long, pencil-like canes of glass for lampworking) and frit (crushed or powdered glass used in fusing and lampworking). These are also identified by COE. Mosaic and stained glass artists don't use frit and seldom use rods.

Cutting Glass

The name of the action, *cutting glass,* is a misnomer; we actually break glass. A glass cutter doesn't *cut* glass, it scores glass, scratching the surface and weakening its structure so that we can break it into the shape we desire. Most glass art studios have two tools for cutting glass: tile nippers and glass cutters. Tools such as running pliers enhance precision, speed, and safety.

Scoring Glass with a Glass Cutter

YOU WILL NEED:

- 4 sheets of plain window glass, each at least 12" × 6" (30 × 15 cm) *Note: Each sheet will be used for one cutting exercise.*
- Glass cutter
- Permanent marker
- Ruler
- Cutting oil in jar
- Cutting pad, larger than the glass
- Safety glasses
- Soft cloth or paper towel
- Pliers
- Blue Runner *(optional)*
- Ring Star (or similar running pliers for curved scores *(optional)*

TIPS FOR SUCCESS:

- Always clean your worktable before laying glass on it—even a small piece of leftover solder or a small shard of glass from a previous project can break your glass sheet when you score a new piece.
- When scoring glass, always start at one edge and draw the score without stopping until you reach another edge.
- Hold the glass cutter straight up with both hands as you pull it across the glass. It's important to be steady; avoid tilting the cutter to either side.
- Apply a slight downward pressure as you pull; too much and you'll hear a tearing or crunching sound; not enough and no score will appear on the glass. The best score leaves a light, continuous line on the glass and produces a slight "snicking" sound. With practice, you'll recognize it.
- Never go over a score to deepen it—it damages your glass cutter.
- Dip the glass cutter in oil between each score.
- The side of the glass with the score is the top. The side of the glass without the score is the underside.

Clockwise from bottom left: sheet glass (blue and beige), assorted lampworking rods, glass powder (yellow), and frit (turquoise)

EXERCISE 1:
Basic Straight Cuts

1. Clean your workboard with the soft cloth or paper towel and put on the safety glasses. Lay the cutting pad on your workboard and put one sheet of window glass on it.

2. Remove the glass cutter from the oil jar. With both hands, reach over the glass to the top edge. Place the blade of the cutter at the edge, centered and resting on the glass.

3. Holding the cutter with both hands, draw it slowly toward you, applying a slight downward pressure. You should hear a "snicking" noise and see a line on the glass where the glass cutter has been. Try to score a straight line down the middle of the glass, without lifting the glass cutter, until you reach the edge nearest you. Lift the glass cutter and return it to the oil jar.

4. If you have a Blue Runner (or similar running pliers for straight scores), slide the glass between the jaws so that the raised blue line on the upper jaw covers the score line. Squeeze until the glass breaks.

5. If you don't have a Blue Runner, hold the glass up and use the pliers to tap the underside of the glass along the score to weaken the score further. Slide the glass toward the edge of the workboard or table so that the score rests on the edge. Grasp the free edge with the pliers as fully as you can, and snap off with a downward motion.

6. Repeat Steps 2–5 with the pieces that remain from the first sheet of glass, dipping the cutter in oil after each score, until you feel that you can score and break a strip of glass cleanly.

7. Rest the cutter in the oil jar. Remove the cutting pad from the workboard and shake it out over a garbage can to remove shards.

2

4

5

EXERCISE 2:
Scoring a Straight Pattern Line

1. Return the cutting pad to your workboard and set a new sheet of window glass on it. With the ruler and permanent marker, draw straight lines down the glass, 1" (2.5 cm) apart. Each line should be 12" (30 cm) long.

2. Place the glass cutter at the top edge on one of the lines. Draw the cutter down the glass, scoring exactly in the center of the marker line. If you find it hard to score a straight line, try standing and taking a step away from the glass as you score, keeping your wrists and forearms stiff.

3. Place the cutter in the jar and break the glass strip from the sheet.

4. Repeat until all the marker lines have been scored and cut.

5. Remove the cutting pad from the workboard and shake it out over a garbage can to remove shards.

ECO·TIP **Conserving Glass**

Art glass is beautiful but expensive, and it behooves us to waste as little as possible. When cutting glass from a pattern, mark and cut one pattern piece at a time and place the pattern as close to the edge of the glass sheet as possible. If you're using irregularly shaped glass left from another project, use the smallest piece possible that will contain the pattern; turn the pattern piece over, if need be, to make it fit. All leftovers should be saved—even a piece as small as the fingernail on your pinky finger might eventually be put to good use in projects such as *Wild Roses* and *Fantastic Journey* (see part 3, "Melding Skills and Techniques: Studio Projects").

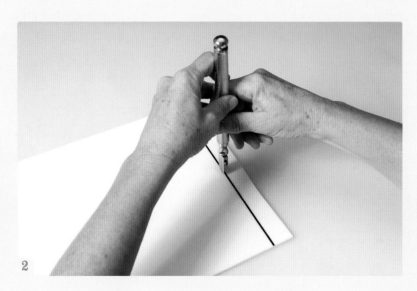

2

Scoring and Breaking a Curve

Scoring a curved line is harder than scoring a straight line; firmness and precision must now be tempered with changes of angle as you pull the glass cutter.

1. Place the cutting pad on your workboard. Lay a new sheet of glass on the cutting pad.

2. With the marker, draw a curve with a gentle *S* shape from top to bottom, along the long edge of the glass.

3. With the cutter, score the *S* down the center of the marker line in one pull. Rest the cutter in the oil jar.

4. If you have a Ring Star (or similar running pliers for curved scores), slide the glass between the jaws so that the cone is under the score line.

5. With slight squeezing motions, apply pressure to the line all along the score. Do *not* press hard. Repeat the squeezing motions along the line until the curved strip separates from the glass sheet.

6. If you don't have a Ring Star (or similar tool), use pliers to gently tap up and down the score line several times. When the score begins to deepen, hold the larger side of the glass sheet in one hand and use the pliers to grab onto the curved strip. Gently wiggle the glass strip; if it doesn't separate from the main sheet, tap the underside of the glass some more. Repeat until the glass separates.

7. Repeat Steps 2–6 until the glass sheet is cut up.

8. Remove the cutting pad from the workboard and shake it out over a garbage can to remove shards.

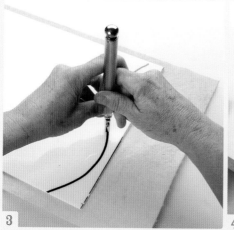
3

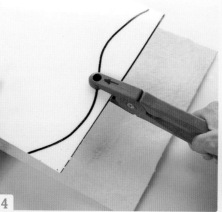
4

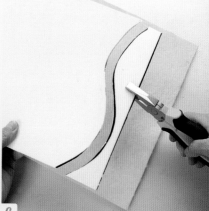
6

EXERCISE 4:
Scoring and Cutting Circles

It's impossible to cut a perfect circle in one score. In this exercise, you'll practice the steps needed to cut a circle of glass.

1. With the marker, draw three circles on the remaining glass sheet.

2. With the marker, draw straight lines from edge to edge between the circles to divide the glass sheet into three pieces. Each piece should have one circle in it.

3. Score the glass sheet along the straight lines you've drawn and open with the Blue Runner.

4. Place one piece with a circle on the cutting pad. With the marker, draw three to four additional cutting lines (shown here as dashed lines) that lead off the circle to the edge of the glass piece.

5. Starting at the edge of the glass, score and break the first cut.

6. Score and break the second cut.

7. Score and break the third cut.

8. With the pliers, remove any small pieces that didn't come off with the score. (This is called *grozing*.)

9. Use the glass grinder to even out any small bumps.

10. Repeat Steps 4–9 until all the circles have been scored and cut.

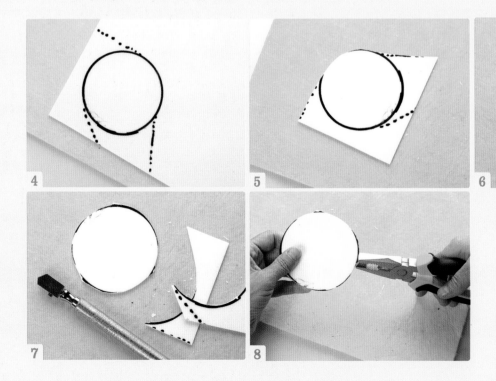

CUTTING ART GLASS

Very seldom is art glass as smooth as window glass. Before marking glass for cuts, check both sides of the glass and always cut on the smoother surface. If you want the other side to be dominant in your work, cut on the smooth side but place the pattern piece upside down before marking the glass.

Drilling Glass

Glass can be drilled with a glass grinder after you replace the grinding bit with a drill bit. It's an exercise in patience because you must work slowly and pause frequently to wet the drill head and the glass to cool and clean them. Work from the underside of the glass. Apply moderate pressure against the drill. Avoid pressing hard as you drill, or you might accidentally slam the glass against the grinder when the bit finally breaks through. Use a light hand to avoid slipping the bit out of the hole you're making, because scratches weaken the glass and cause cracks.

Grinding head (left); drill head (right)

Making Flower Petals with a Tile Nipper

It's quick and easy to use a tile nipper and art glass scraps to make flower petals such as those used in the Dahlia project (in part 2, chapter 3, "Stained Glass") and in the aforementioned Wild Roses project (in part 3, "Melding Skills and Techniques: Studio Projects"). Work over a garbage can to catch messy bits of broken glass.

1. Select several large glass scraps that look good together. With the tile nipper, break them into pieces that are about 2" × 1" (5 × 2.5 cm). Precise measurements or shapes aren't important.

2. Pick up one piece of glass. With the tile nipper, taper the piece toward one end. Place the small end of the petal between the nipper disks, close to the edge of the glass. Squeeze the handles until a sliver of glass breaks off. The tapered end should now curve inward.

3. Using the tile nipper, work your way around the wider end of the glass to shape and round the top of the petal. I often urge my students to "think like a rabbit"—that is, use the tile nipper to nibble away the glass in very small bites.

4. Grind the petal with the grinder to smooth the edges. Wash and dry.

Steps 1-3, from left to right

Stained
Glass

Traditional leaded stained glass windows are pieced together like a flat puzzle. Each piece is fitted into a channel of pure lead, called came. The lead is soldered at the corners, locking in the glass. The artist designs the puzzle, cuts the pieces, and fits them together. Sometimes the pieces are painted with fine details that can't be rendered otherwise. The technique is hundreds of years old and is still practiced today.

In the nineteenth century, a new technique called *copper foiling* was developed. This technique replaced the traditional lead came with a very thin layer of copper and a belt of lead and tin solder. Copper foiling offered new possibilities in shape, size, and detailing, and is the technique used for the projects in this book.

Common Stained Glass Processes

CREATING AND USING PATTERNS

For simple stained glass creations, creating a pattern is like drawing a puzzle. You define the outer dimensions of the piece you wish to create, and then divide the inside into shapes and colors. Pieces that are very small or very narrow need not be included because the copper foil will cover them and no glass will be visible; it's easier

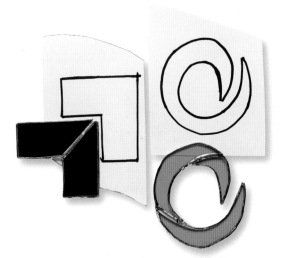

LEFT Inside corners can't be cut without breaking; one solution is to cut the piece evenly into two pieces. Spirals must be cut into several parts to accommodate the curves. Using one color of glass in a composite construction such as these makes solder seams less noticeable.

The same pattern was used to cut two pieces from the same sheet of glass. The piece on the left takes advantage of the visual flow of the glass colors.

to leave a gap between pieces and fill it in with solder. There are some shapes that can't be cut—inside angles, and very sharp curves, for instance. If you wish to include those shapes in your design, divide them into several pieces.

Once you have your pattern defined, copy it to pattern paper and trace it with a marker. Mark each pattern piece with the color you wish to use. If your design has a directional flow that you wish to emphasize (e.g., the curve of a leaf), and you'll be using glass that has color flowing through it unevenly, mark the piece to show which direction the design should run.

Cut the outside borders of the pattern with regular scissors and the rest with pattern shears. If the edges of the pattern pieces don't cut cleanly, use regular scissors to trim off the extra bits.

If you've drawn your design on pattern paper from the start, photocopy or photograph the pattern before you cut it up so that you can use it as a guide for putting together the glass pieces before soldering.

CUTTING GLASS

Cutting glass is an important skill that all glass artists must master if they wish to express themselves in mosaic, stained glass, or fusing. Instruction on how to cut glass and a series of exercises to help you learn and practice this skill can be found at the beginning of part 2.

GRINDING GLASS

The purpose of grinding is to remove glass splinters and roughen up the edge of the glass so that copper foil will adhere well to it. Every piece to be included in your creation must be ground, washed, and dried.

If you have an electric grinder, put on safety glasses and fill the grinder's reservoir with water. When you start the grinder, a small wave of water should push up against the drill head; if not, add more water. This wave is important—it will prevent the glass and the grinder from overheating and will wash powdery glass residue down into the reservoir where it won't be a health risk. The reservoir must be cleaned occasionally to remove the accumulated glass sludge; the water level should be topped off every time you use the grinder.

To grind, lay the glass piece flat on the surface of the grinder. Slide it forward until the rim of the glass makes contact with the drill head. Using both hands and light to mild pressure only, grind the edge of the glass piece by turning it against the drill head until the entire perimeter has been ground. Don't slide your finger against the glass rim to see whether the grinding has been effective; instead, dry the piece and examine the rim. The ground rim should appear white, almost chalky. If it still appears bright and shiny, grind it again. After grinding, wash the piece with dishwashing liquid and water, and dry.

If you don't have a grinder, grind the edges of your glass pieces with a grinding stone. Hold the stone and the glass under water and rub the edges of the glass with the stone in small, circular motions. Dry the piece and examine the edge. Repeat until the entire edge is ground well. After grinding, wash the piece with dishwashing liquid and water, and dry.

Two pieces of the same glass: The bottom piece is freshly cut, and the edges of the top piece have been ground.

Foiling and Burnishing

Each piece of glass for your creation must be wrapped in copper foil before soldering. Many nonglass items, such as stones, must also be foiled to provide a base for the solder.

YOU WILL NEED:

- 1 roll of copper foil, ¼" wide or similar
- 1 piece of glass, ground, washed, and dried
- Burnisher

TECHNIQUE:

1. Open the roll of copper foil. If this is a new roll, remove the first layer of copper foil and throw it away if it's discolored.

2. Pull about 6" (15 cm) of copper foil from the roll (more if you'll be foiling more than one or two pieces). Tear the strip from the rest of the roll, for convenience.

3. Peel away a bit of paper from one end of the copper strip. This should expose the underside of the copper. The underside will be sticky with adhesive.

4. Holding the glass piece so that the rim faces you, stick the underside of the copper foil to the rim of glass so that the foil is centered, with an equal amount of excess copper hanging over both sides of the rim. Press the copper firmly to the glass rim.

5. Peel off more paper from the copper strip. Rotate the glass, pressing the copper onto the rim, until the circumference of the glass is covered, plus an overlap of at least ¼" (½ cm). Press the copper firmly to the rim with your fingers.

6. With your fingers, press the excess copper onto the sides of the glass.

7. With the burnisher, using a back and forth movement, gently rub the copper foil on the rim until it's fully adhered to the glass. It should feel very smooth.

8. Turn the glass and rub the copper foil around the edge of the glass until it's firmly adhered and very smooth to the touch. Repeat on the other side.

Soldering

Solder creates a strong metal belt around and between our glass pieces to hold them together.

MATERIALS

- 3 or 4 pieces of art glass, ground and foiled
- Flux
- Solder

TOOLS

- Cotton rag or sock (soldering rag)
- Dishwashing liquid, water
- Flux brush
- Flux in a small dish
- Soldering iron

1. Place the foiled art glass on your worktable so that the edges are touching. Turn on your soldering iron. Wet the soldering rag and squeeze out the excess water. Place the dampened rag on your workboard.

2. Wipe the tip of the soldering iron on the damp rag to clean it. Touch it to the end of the solder and see if the solder melts instantly. If not, wait a minute and try again. When the solder melts easily, the soldering iron is hot enough to be used.

Tack-Soldering One Side to Freeze the Glass Arrangement

3. Verify that all the glass pieces are arranged exactly as desired. With the flux brush, wipe flux onto the copper seams between the pieces. Hold the solder stick over a copper seam. With the hot tip of the soldering iron, melt a drop of solder onto the copper. It should adhere to both sides of the seam.

4. Tack-solder between all the seams. If the pieces are large or the design is complex, tack-solder at least two places along each seam. All the glass pieces should now be soldered into location.

TIP	**Tips for Soldering Success**

- Flux is a salt compound that helps solder adhere to copper. It can sting or irritate your skin; if you find it bothersome, wear latex gloves.

- The soldering iron and the solder will be very hot while in use, and for some time afterward. Always rest the iron on a proper metal holder when not in use. See "Safety First," in part 1, chapter 2, for more tips on soldering safety.

- The tip of the soldering iron should be cleaned on the damp rag periodically as you work. If it doesn't pick up solder, the soldering tip is either too cool or too dirty.

- Solder seams should be thick and rounded on top, not flat, and should have clean edges.

From left to right: a soldering iron on a metal stand, pieces of foiled glass, a soldering rag (before dampening), and several sticks of solder

4

5

8

Full Soldering

5. Holding the solder stick next to the copper, melt more solder into and onto all the seams on the top of the construction. Try not to touch the glass with the soldering iron, as this can overheat the glass and break it. If the solder appears uneven, hold the soldering iron against the solder's surface for a moment to melt it again. The seams should appear smooth and rounded on top. If they're flat, add more solder to thicken them. Let the piece cool before continuing.

6. Turn the piece over. Wipe flux onto the seams, and full-solder the entire back of the piece. (There's no need to tack-solder the back.) If you hold the iron to the seams for too long, the solder might melt out the other side; if this happens, repair it after soldering the back. Let the piece cool before continuing.

7. Turn the glass over. If drips melted through, touch them briefly with the soldering iron to melt them back into the piece or to remove them. Fill in any gaps that developed when you soldered the back. Let the piece cool.

8. Hold the glass so that the rim is facing up. With a light touch, apply solder to the entire rim and to any unsoldered open spaces. Keep your hands away from the area you're working on. If the glass is very hot, either let it cool or grasp it with the damp soldering rag as you work.

9. After the piece has cooled, scrub it with an old toothbrush dipped in dishwashing liquid and water. Rinse and dry.

TIP | Using Lead-Free Solder

Lead-free solder doesn't melt as easily as regular solder. If you find that you're leaving little peaks of metal when you full-solder, hold the tack-soldered glass with a rag or jewelry pliers and change the angle you're working at. If you work at a slower pace, you'll be able to melt more of the solder before you lift the iron.

Finishing Techniques

APPLYING PATINA

Always wear latex gloves and a protective apron when applying patina to soldered seams; patina is an acid and can burn your skin and will discolor your clothing. (It doesn't harm glass.) To apply patina, soak a cotton ball with patina and wipe on the seams.

To strengthen the color, rub the seam with the cotton ball. Set the piece aside for twenty minutes. After twenty minutes, gently wash the entire piece with dishwashing liquid, water, and an old toothbrush, paying special attention to the seams. Dry very well before apply finishing compound.

APPLYING FINISHING COMPOUND

Finishing oil or wax seals the soldered seams and prevents unsightly and harmful corrosion. Apply with a cotton ball after all the seams are thoroughly dry. A little oil goes a very long way; as the seams accept the oil, they will become shinier, particularly if they have been treated with patina. If oil on the glass bothers you, wipe it off with a dry tissue. Follow the instructions on the bottle of finishing wax to buff and polish it. Don't wash the piece after adding finishing compound.

WASHING AND DRYING

Washing is best carried out with an old toothbrush and a little dishwashing liquid. Depending on the stage of the project, the dishwashing liquid is needed to remove traces of adhesive, cutting oil, flux, or acids. Used toothbrushes are excellent for getting into small places and can gently scrub without scarring solder or removing patina.

More Than Glass

It's possible to include other materials in stained glass creations; indeed, anything that won't melt or burn from the heat of the soldering iron can be used. While some metals, such as copper, can be soldered directly into the piece, most items must be wrapped with copper foil. In many cases it isn't necessary to grind the edges first. Common inclusions include stones (polished or unpolished; see the *Wild Roses* project in part 3, and the *Open-Topped Agate Box* project in part 2, chapter 3), wood, shells (see the *At the Beach* project in part 2 chapter 3), and metal.

ECO·TIP Flea Market Finds

Three well-known Rs of recycling are Reduce, Reuse, and Recycle. Before you run out to buy something new, visit garage sales and flea markets to see if you can find something old that you can give new life to in your studio or artwork. Lucky finds can include lantern frames, lamp bases, antique glassware, and items that can add atmosphere to your studio or can display finished pieces.

Working with Wire

Very thin wire, such as jewelry wire, can be soldered into stained glass without preparation. But thicker wire—wire thin enough to be manipulated with pliers but thick enough to hold its shape and support your work—must be prepared with a coat of solder ahead of time because the process of superheating the wire before applying solder can crack glass if done in situ.

MATERIALS

- Metal wire, moderate to heavy weight
- Flux
- Solder

TOOLS

- Cotton rag or sock (soldering rag)
- Flux brush
- Jewelry pliers or regular pliers
- Metal snips
- Permanent marker
- Soldering iron

1. With the metal snips, cut off a piece of wire.

2. With the pliers, shape the wire.

3. Lay the wire against the soldered seam where you wish to solder it. Mark just inside the boundaries with a permanent marker.

Clockwise, from upper right: a roll of wire, two pairs of pliers, solder sticks, a soldering iron, metal snips, and a soldering rag (before dampening)

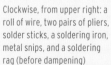

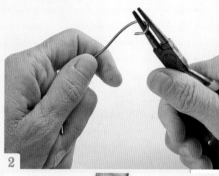

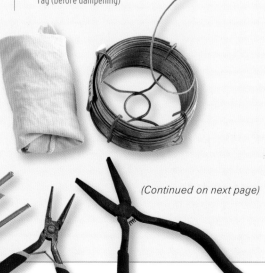

(Continued on next page)

Working with Wire (Continued)

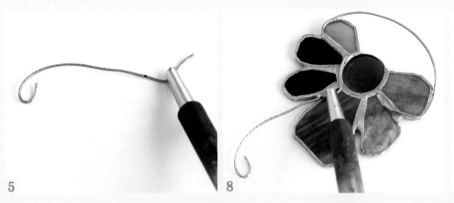

A wire with a large ceramic bead was added to this flower. The end of the wire was capped with a decorative drop of lead to prevent the bead from falling off.

4. Place the metal on your workboard. Wipe with flux between the marks.

5. Lay the hot soldering iron against the wire and hold it there until the wire changes color from heat. Brush on more flux and apply solder to the wire between the marks.

6. If the solder doesn't stick, superheat the wire again and add more flux.

7. Using the pliers, turn the wire over and repeat Steps 5 and 6. Let cool. Place the prepared wire against the seam where it will be soldered.

8. With a light touch and no flux, solder the wire into the seam.

Adding Beads

Beads can be added to your work in several ways; string them onto a dangling tail or a hanging wire, slide them on wire that's soldered into your work, or wrap them in copper foil and solder. If you string beads on wire, you must consider how you'll prevent them from falling off; you can curve the wire with pliers or add a drop of solder to the end of the wire.

Safety Alert! – Working with Lead

Lead came comes in long strips and several shapes. Came is pure lead, easily cut and melted, and toxic if ingested. You'll find that your hands are discolored after working with lead; this is lead residue on your skin. Be sure to wash well with a soap that removes metal residue when you finish working, and before you eat, drink, smoke, or touch another person. Lead is soft and can easily be cut with metal snips. Store came out of the reach of children, and discard any cut bits immediately.

Making Hinges

FOR STAINED GLASS PROJECTS

The components used to make hinges for stained glass work look like long spaghetti made of brass. They have two parts: the outer tubing and the inner rod. Hinges are commonly used to construct lidded boxes but have additional applications. For an example of how hinges can be used a project, see the *Stained Glass Hibiscus Treasure Box* project in part 3.

1. Lay the outer tubing along the side of the box base where the lid will turn on the hinge. With a permanent marker, mark the outer tubing about ½" (1.3 cm) shorter than the box's width.

2. Slide the inner rod into the outer tubing. Using a sharp tool, such as a small saw blade, gently saw through the outer tubing at the spot you marked until you can see a definite trench with an open hole in the metal.

3. Remove the inner rod.

The tools for making hinges for stained glass work are very simple: left to right, ruler, brass hinge parts, and a small jigsaw blade.

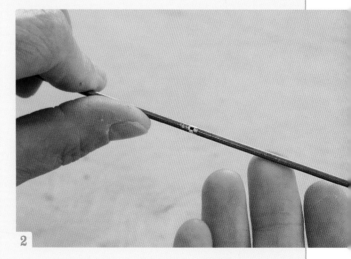

(Continued on next page)

Making Hinges *(Continued)*

4. Continue sawing until you've cut through at least one-quarter of the tubing's diameter.

5. Grasp the tubing in both hands, on either side of the cut with the cut facing away from you. Press with your thumbs and quickly snap the hinge along the cut.

6. With a metal file, smooth any snags from the cut end.

7. Slide the rod into the cut end. If it sticks, use a pointed tool such as needle-nosed pliers or a fork tine to round the tube opening from the inside. Repeat until the rod can smoothly slide into the outer tubing. Remove the inner rod and set aside.

8. Apply flux to all of the tubing except the very ends. Hold the tubing with pliers and rest the hot soldering iron on the tubing until the brass takes on a reddish shade. Apply a thin layer of solder to all the tubing except the last ¼" (½ cm) of each end. Apply more flux as needed. Work from the center outward and stop ¼" (½ cm) from the edge to avoid getting solder inside the tubing ends.

9. Let the tubing cool. Wash it with dishwashing liquid and water or wipe it down with a wet cloth and dry. Set aside.

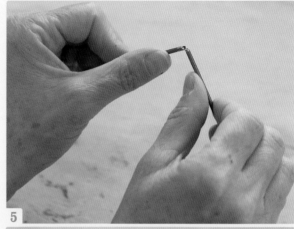

10. To form the hinge arms, cut the inner rod at the center to make two smaller rods. The cut ends (from the center) will be slightly flattened.

11. Slide the uncut ends of the rods into the shortened tubing so that they meet in the middle. One inch (2.5 cm) of rod should stick out on each side of the tubing. If the rods are too long, shorten them from the cut end.

12. Hold one piece of rod close to the cut end. With your other hand, gently bend the rest of the rod over your thumb to form a right angle. The short arm of the angle should be 1" (2.5 cm) long, and should include the cut end of the rod.

13. Apply flux to the short arm of the rod. Heat the brass and apply a thin layer of solder from the cut end to the bend in the hinge arm. Let it cool before washing it with dishwashing liquid and water and drying.

14. Repeat steps 12–13 to prepare the second rod.

15. Slide the long, unsoldered arms of the rods into the tubing to complete the hinge.

Safety Alert!

Brass won't take solder well unless it is *very* hot, and it transmits that heat very quickly! To avoid burning your fingers, always handle hot brass with pliers. If you've been working on a piece of brass and need to pick it up to reposition it, swipe it first with a damp cloth to cool the metal.

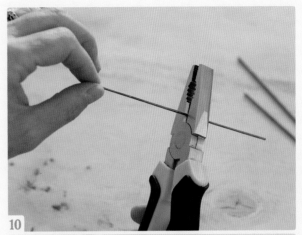

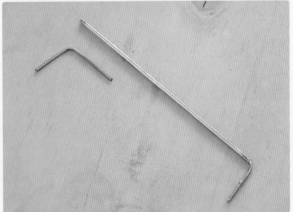

Good Design Practices

Follow these tips to make your stained glass constructions stronger:

- **Foiling:** To make invisible foil seams, plan the overlap of the beginning and end of the copper foil wrap for an area that will be inside a seam. In a large construction, all the inside pieces will be soldered all around. But in a construction such as a flower, many of the glass edges will be exposed, so the overlap should be made at the base curve of the petal.

- **Shapes that can't be cut:** As noted earlier, some shapes can't be cut, but you can include them in your design anyway by adding extra cutting lines to the pattern. See the examples on the opening page of this chapter to learn how this can be done.

- **Straight vs. curved:** Curved lines are much stronger than straight lines. Avoid including straight lines that run from one edge to another. A straight edge-to-edge seam is a weak seam that invites your panel or window to bend or even snap in half. If the design calls for straight lines, intersect them before reaching the edge of the panel.

Troubleshooting and Making Repairs

The following tips will help you troubleshoot and make repairs, whether due to error or accident:

- **Foil is loose:** Foil won't stick to glass that is wet, oily, or dirty. Remove the foil, wash the glass well with dishwashing liquid and water, and dry it completely. Wash and dry your hands as well. Refoil the piece. If the foil still won't stick, remove the foil and regrind the piece.

- **Solder won't stick:** Solder won't stick to copper if there's insufficient flux, so applying more flux to the copper foil should be your first step. If solder still doesn't stick well, the copper foil may have folded over when you burnished—solder won't stick to the gluey underside of copper foil. If the area without solder is small, let it cool, then dab more solder on the top of the gap while holding a damp cloth very close to the seam as you work; it will cool the solder, which will solidify faster and fill the gap.

- **Solder is stuck on glass:** Unless the solder is an extension of a seam, it should wash off or peel off the glass when you're washing the finished project. If it's physically connected to a seam, add flux and melt it off with a light touch of the soldering iron.

- **Foil is torn:** Sometimes foil will separate at the seams or tear during soldering after most of the piece has been done, when it's too much trouble to remove the piece and start over. If this happens, finish soldering the construction carefully to prevent the loose glass from falling out. Wash the piece and dry it very well. If the loose or torn foil can be left, do so, and burnish flat. If the loose foil is torn or twisted, remove it. Take a strip of new foil from the copper foil roll, and apply it to the gap with an overlap of at least 1" (2.5 cm) on either side. Burnish very well to adhere the copper fully to the existing solder, as well as the glass. Apply flux sparingly, and tack-solder the two ends in place before soldering the rest. When all is soldered, return to the tacked ends; wipe the soldering iron from the inside toward the edges, and continue onto the already soldered area to form a seamless join.

- **A piece is missing:** When making large panels with many parts, pieces can be misplaced or accidentally cut up. If you discover that you're missing a piece after you've started soldering, tack and full-solder

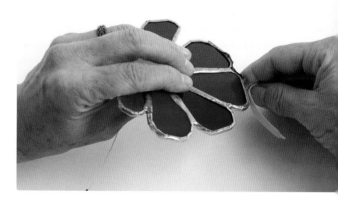

Layer the new foil over the torn section after washing and drying the solder you've already applied. Even a miniscule tear should be repaired.

the front, leaving the gap. Wipe the panel clean with a paper towel or slightly damp cloth. Place a piece of glass under the gap, and trace the shape with a permanent marker. Prepare the piece and drop it into place. Apply flux and solder the seams.

- **Pieces are too big:** When making panels, every piece must be exactly the right size or the design will distort. If you discover that the pieces don't fit inside the design after foiling, lift the largest piece from the design. Rearrange the pieces. If they all fit together now as they should, tack-solder them into place, leaving a gap for the large piece you removed. (If they don't fit together, lift another piece.) After tack-soldering, lay the large piece over the gap and mark the glass where you need to trim it so that it will fit into the gap. Remove the copper foil only from the area that must be trimmed, plus a little extra. Cut the glass and grind the exposed edges. If the glass piece now fits in the gap (with a little room to spare, for the foil), foil the newly cut edge, drop the piece into the gap, and continue soldering the panel. If the piece still doesn't fit, trim again as needed. Repeat until the piece fits into the gap.

- **A small crack has formed:** Hairline cracks that don't threaten the structural integrity of the piece can be created or discovered during soldering. If you wish to hide them, and the design allows for it, after fully soldering the piece on both sides, wash and dry the glass to remove all dirt, flux, oil, and water. Adhere a strip of copper foil from one seam to the next, covering the crack, on one side of your construction. Burnish well. Apply flux sparingly and solder, using the technique described earlier in this list, in the "Foil is torn" entry. Turn the piece over and apply another strip of copper foil to the back of the crack.

- **Glass has broken:** Repairing stained glass panels often requires replacing glass, and any piece with a serious crack should be replaced, for structural and aesthetic reasons. Clean the area to be worked on. If the glass is shattered, but still intact, bang it with pliers a bit on both sides of the panel to loosen it up. If the crack is minimal (or if there's some other reason for replacing the piece), score the piece several

This stained glass panel was dropped and requires extensive repairs along the top and bottom. After the broken glass is replaced, the panel will look as good as or better than it did before the accident.

times from different directions before banging the underside of the glass. Repeat this until you can remove all the glass with the pliers. Most likely, the copper foil will be left behind; it should be removed with a hot soldering iron.

1. Melt the soldered seam with the soldering iron and hold the iron against the loose foil.

2. Grasp the copper foil with pliers and pull it gently into the gap until it separates from the construction.

3. If the solder is thick and keeps running back onto the copper foil, hold the panel up as you work (or have someone hold it for you). Work from underneath and shake the panel to encourage the excess solder to drop to the workboard.

   Once the old copper foil has been removed, even up or clean the solder from the gap, clean the workboard of all solder drips, and proceed with the technique described earlier in this list, in the entry "A piece is missing."

Stained Glass Flower: Dahlia

Practice your stained glass skills by making a flowery suncatcher to hang in your window. This is a project that you can enjoy many times because the results will always be unique.

MATERIALS

- 1 large glass nugget or other suitable round centerpiece
- Enough art glass scraps to make eight petals, each at least 3" × 3" (7.5 × 7.5 cm)
- Copper foil
- Mid-weight steel wire, at least 5" (12.5 cm)
- Flux
- Solder
- Patina (optional)
- Finishing compound
- 16" (40.5 cm) of jewelry wire, lace, or ribbon
- 4 crimp beads, if using jewelry wire

TOOLS

- Burnisher
- Cotton balls
- Flux brush
- Glass grinder
- Pliers
- Soldering iron
- Soldering rag
- Tile nipper

SKILLS REVIEW

- "Making Flower Petals with a Tile Nipper," *page 49*
- "Foiling and Burnishing," *page 53*
- "Soldering," *page 54*
- "Working with Wire," *page 57*

INSTRUCTIONS

Prepare the Pattern

1. With the tile nipper, break the glass into eight pieces that are about 2" × 1" (5 × 2.5 cm) in size. Shape each piece into a petal.

2. Grind, wash with dishwashing liquid, and dry each piece.

3. Select one petal. Starting at the base, wrap the petal edge in copper foil. Overlap the beginning and end by at least ½" (1.3 cm). Press the foil to the glass and burnish. Repeat until you've foiled and burnished all the petals.

4. Wash and dry the centerpiece. Wrap it in copper foil. Burnish.

(Continued on next page)

1

3

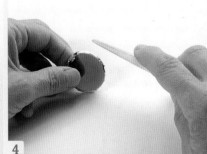

4

5

7

9

10

11

5. Place the centerpiece in the center of your workboard. Arrange five or six petals around the centerpiece, with the tapered base against the centerpiece. The petals should be close to each other, without large gaps at the base.

Make the Flower

6. Turn on the soldering iron and dampen the soldering rag. Test the iron against a piece of solder. When the solder melts quickly, the iron is hot enough to use.

7. With the flux brush, apply flux to the sides of the petals, near the centerpiece. Tack-solder the petals to the centerpiece and to each other.

8. Apply flux to all the visible copper. Full-solder the top, filling any gaps between the nugget and the petals with solder and putting extra solder at the base of the petals to bridge between them. Let the flower cool.

9. Turn the flower over. Apply flux and full-solder the back. Let cool.

10. Hold the flower with the petal rims up. With a light hand, run solder all along the rims. Be sure to coat the copper everywhere, including between the petals. If the gap between petals is too small for the soldering iron, fill the gap with solder, then shake the hot solder out onto the table while it's still melted. Let the flower cool.

Add the Metal Hanging Loop

11. Bend the midweight wire at the center. Place it against the back of the flower. With the pliers, curl or curve the ends of the wire so that they cup the sides of the centerpiece.

13

14

15

19

12. Flux, superheat, and coat the ends of the wire. To avoid burns, don't touch the wire with your fingers; use the pliers instead. Let the wire cool.

13. Turn the flower facedown, and put the prepared wire against the back of the centerpiece. Tack-solder one side of the wire to the flower.

14. Check the flower from the front—is the wire loop centered? If so, proceed. If not, adjust the location by widening or narrowing the angle of the loop until you're satisfied with the shape of the wire loop.

15. Solder the free end of the wire to the back of the flower. Let the solder cool and harden, then full-solder the other side. Add enough solder to the ends of the wire to round them off. Let the flower cool.

16. Scrub the flower with dishwashing liquid and water. Dry well.

17. If patina is desired, apply with a cotton ball, wait twenty minutes, and repeat Step 16.

18. Apply finishing compound with a cotton ball.

Add the Hanging Wire

19. If you have jewelry wire and crimp beads, slide two crimp beads onto one end of the jewelry wire. Thread this end through the metal loop at the top of the flower. Fold about 1" (2.5 cm) of the wire back over, enclosing the metal hanging loop. Slide the beads over the loose end of the wire and squeeze firmly shut with the pliers. Tug on the crimp beads a bit to check that they're securely closed.

20. Slide two crimp beads onto the other end of the jewelry wire. Fold over about 2" (5 cm) of wire. Slide the crimp beads onto the loose end of the wire and squeeze shut, to make a loop.

21. If you don't have jewelry wire, tie one end of the length of lace, cord, or ribbon to the loop of the flower. Tie a loop and knot at the other end.

Open-Topped
Agate Box

This opened-topped box teaches the techniques of creating box bases and other 3-D objects in stained glass. The box makes a lovely trinket box or a nice, personal accent in an office environment. Because patina will roughen and possibly discolor the agate, this piece is left with silver-colored seams.

MATERIALS

- 1 square of art glass, any color, 3" × 3" (7.5 × 7.5 cm)
- 3 rectangles of art glass, any color, 3" × 1½" (7.5 × 4 cm)
- 1 rectangle of clear window glass, 3" × 1½" (7.5 × 4 cm)
- 1 polished agate slab, about 3" × 2" (7.5 × 5 cm)
- Copper foil
- Flux
- Solder
- Finishing compound

TOOLS

- Burnisher
- Cutting pad
- Flux brush
- Glass cutter
- Permanent marker
- Soldering iron
- Soldering rag

SKILLS REVIEW

- "Foiling and Burnishing," page 53
- "Soldering," page 54

INSTRUCTIONS

Construct the Box

1. Grind the glass square. Wash it with dishwashing liquid and water to remove any cutting oil. Dry well. This will be the box floor.

2. Grind the four rectangles, grinding each of the short sides six times to slightly shorten the rectangles. Wash them with dishwashing liquid and water to remove any cutting oil. Dry well. These will be the box walls.

3. Foil all the glass pieces and the agate. The foil overlap on the rectangles should be made on the short sides.

The creative materials needed to make the box: (top) glass, (lower left) a sliced and polished agate, and (lower right) a roll of copper foil

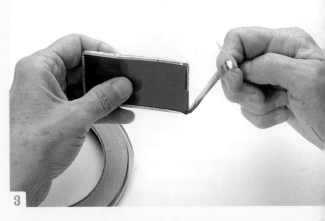

(Continued on next page)

4. Set the square and the agate aside. Examine the rectangles; if the sides of each piece look different or are textured, decide which side of the glass will face outward and which will be on the inside of the box. With the marker, mark the inside with an *X*.

5. Examine the rectangles again. On the same side as the *X*, mark a *T* near the straightest of the long sides on each piece. This will indicate which edge will be at the top of the box.

6. Turn on the soldering iron and dampen the soldering rag. Brush flux onto the edges of each rectangle. Apply a light coating of flux to the copper foil. Turn the rectangles over and repeat.

7. Do not solder the rims.

8. Pick out two rectangles. Stand them on their long edge at a 90-degree angle, with the *X* marks on the inside of the angle and the *T* mark at the bottom. Position them with their corners touching but not overlapping. This is the strongest corner seam possible.

9. Tack a bit of solder at the top of the joint, where the rectangles meet. Examine the angle. Is it 90 degrees? If not, gently adjust it.

10. Tack-solder the joint at the outside and inside of the angle, at the workboard level. Let cool.

11. Repeat Step 10 with the remaining rectangles.

12. Set up the walls so that they're *T* side down and parallel to each other.

13. Set the base on one set of walls so that there's some overlap of the base onto the wall. Flux the copper seams and tack-solder the base to one set of walls.

14. Move the other wall set so that it's now resting under the unsoldered sides of the base. Adjust its location so that the base extends just a little over the edge of the walls, while the side joints meet up. Don't worry if there are slight gaps between the glass pieces or if there's a bit of overlap. This is the result of small differences in size between the pieces or minor differences in angles. Tack-solder the base to the one side of the new walls.

15. Gently move the unattached wall if its location should be adjusted. Tack-solder the second wall.

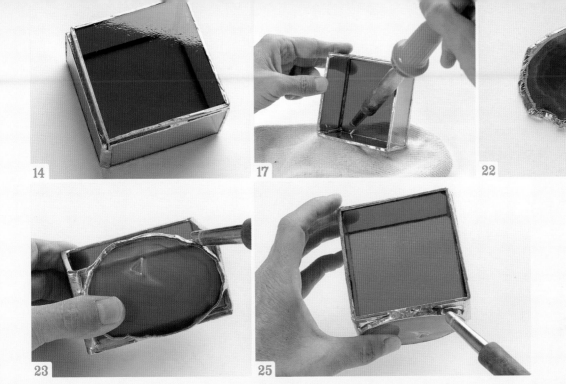

16. Turning the box so that the seam being worked on is always on top, full-solder the side and base joints together, if they meet. Don't attempt to solder joints with big gaps yet.

17. Turn the box around so that the inside is facing you. Solder together all the seams and cover all the copper foil on the inside of the box. If there are gaps between the pieces, rest the open edge on a damp cloth and add solder; the solder will cool and solidify faster and will fill the gap.

18. Complete soldering of the outside seams and fix any lumps of melted solder.

19. Set the box upside down. Add a bit of flux, and apply solder to the copper foil on the bottom of the box floor.

20. Set the box right side up. With a light hand, apply a layer of solder to the top edge of the box to even the seams.

21. After the box cools, wash with dishwashing liquid and water, taking care to scrub the ink marks off the inside glass surfaces. Dry well and set aside.

Add the Agate

22. Apply flux sparingly to the copper foil on the agate. Solder all the foil (front, back, and rim). Wash the agate with dishwashing liquid and water and dry well.

23. Set the box on the workboard, open side up, with the clear rectangle facing you. Hold the agate against the clear glass so that it, too, rests on the workboard. Without applying flux, tack the agate's seams to the box top edges where they touch on both sides of the agate. Hold the soldering iron a moment against the solder to smooth the seam.

24. If the agate touches the side seams, solder the agate to the corners without flux.

25. Turn the box over; without adding flux, solder the bottom edge of the agate to the bottom of the clear box wall.

26. With a damp cloth, wipe any dirt or stains from areas just soldered. Dry well.

27. Apply finishing compound.

Decorative Panel:

STAINED GLASS PROJECT ## At the Beach

The design of this easy-to-make decorative stained glass panel includes textured glass, nugget inclusions, and strong lead borders. Its colors bring to mind a summer day, clean sand, and a sparkling sea. Enhance the illusion by adding some real seashells, if you wish.

MATERIALS

- Pattern paper
- 1 sheet of typing paper (standard size)
- Art glass, one sheet each:
  Transparent light blue, 9" × 4" (23 × 10 cm)
  Transparent dark blue, 9" × 8" (23 × 20.5 cm)
  Opaque sandy beige, mottled or wavy colors, 9" × 6" (23 × 15 cm)
- 25 glass nuggets in blue, turquoise, green, and purple
- Lead "U" came, at least 50" (130 cm)
- Flat lead ribbon, at least 20" (51 cm)
- Copper foil
- Flux
- Solder
- Patina (black)
- Finishing compound
- Shells *(optional)*

TOOLS

- Burnisher
- Cotton balls
- Cutting pad
- Flux brush
- Glass cutter
- Latex gloves
- Metal snips
- Pattern shears
- Pencil/eraser/ruler
- Permanent/waterproof marker
- Pliers
- Scissors
- Soldering iron
- Soldering rag

SKILLS REVIEW

- "Selecting Glass," *page 42*
- "Cutting Glass," *page 43*
- "Creating and Using Patterns," *page 50*
- "Foiling and Burnishing," *page 53*
- "Soldering," *page 54*

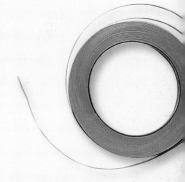

The materials required include: (above) copper foil, (below) sheets of art glass, (below, left) nuggets and shells, and (below, right) solder sticks.

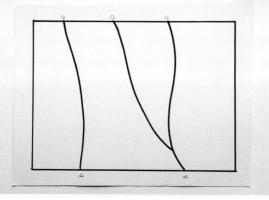

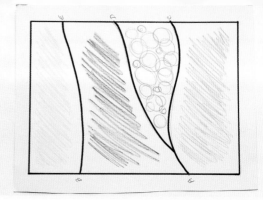

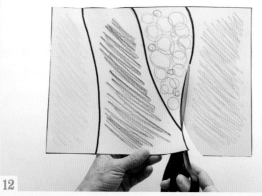

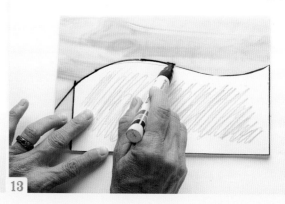

INSTRUCTIONS

Create the Pattern

1. Using the typing sheet as a template, trace a rectangle onto the pattern paper.

2. On the left edge of the pattern, mark one point 3" (7.5 cm) from the bottom-left corner (label A), and a second point 9" (23 cm) from the bottom-left corner (label B).

3. On the right edge of the pattern, mark one point 4" (10 cm) from the bottom-right corner (label C), a second point 7" (18 cm) from the bottom-right corner (label D), and a third point 10" (25.5 cm) from the bottom-right corner (label E).

4. Draw a wavy line from A to C.

5. From point A, move 1" (2.5 cm) to the right along the line you've drawn. Draw a curved line from this point to D.

6. Draw a gentle curve from B to E.

7. Trace all the lines with the marker.

8. Mark the bottom piece as sandy beige and the top piece as light blue.

9. Mark the wedge over the sandy beige as nuggets and the remaining piece as dark blue.

10. Copy the pattern to the typing paper and mark the colors. Set this pattern copy aside.

11. Cut out the rectangle of pattern paper using regular scissors.

12. Cut the pattern pieces out with pattern shears.

Construct the Panel

Before cutting any glass, clean off your workboard and cover it with a cutting pad.

13. Trace the pattern for the sandy beige piece onto the beige glass. Cut the shape from the glass.

14. Trace the pattern for the light blue piece onto the light blue glass. Cut the shape from the glass.

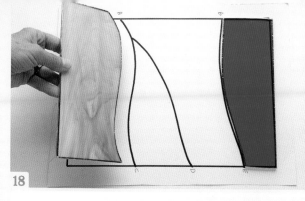

18

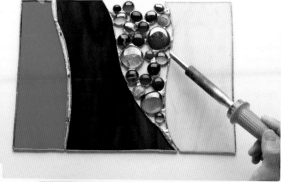

21

22

23

15. Trace the pattern for the dark blue piece onto the dark blue glass. Cut the shape from the glass.

16. Grind all the pieces. Wash them with dishwashing liquid and water. Dry them well.

17. Retrieve the pattern copy and place it on the work-board. Turn on the soldering iron.

18. Wrap the edges of the glass pieces with copper foil. Press the foil to the glass and burnish. As each piece is completed, place it on the pattern copy, in its proper location.

19. Wash all the nuggets with dishwashing liquid and water. Dry them well.

20. Wrap all the nuggets with copper foil and burnish.

21. Arrange the nuggets in the gap between the dark blue and the sandy beige glass. Each nugget should be flat on the workboard. Apply flux sparingly and tack-solder the larger pieces into place, staying far from the borders of the panel. Brush flux onto the nuggets and tack-solder the nuggets into the panel by dripping solder between them.

22. Apply more flux and full-solder the front of the panel, filling in the gaps between the nuggets with solder. Leave about ½" (1 cm) of copper seams unsoldered toward the edges, and don't solder the edges. Let cool.

23. Turn the panel over, facedown. It won't lay flat because the nuggets are larger than the art glass around them. To support the panel, hold its surface flat, and prevent it from bending as you work, slip glass scraps (without copper foil) under the edges of the panel.

24. Apply flux and full-solder the back, leaving about ½" (1 cm) of copper unsoldered toward the edges. Don't solder the edges or the rim of the panel.

25. Turn the panel over to face front. With the hot soldering iron, melt and clean up any solder drips or bubbles.

(Continued on next page)

Stretching and Cutting Lead Came and Ribbon

Lead came and ribbon must be stretched before use or they will eventually sag off a panel. Before stretching came, lay it out as straight as possible. If it has twisted or the edges are bent, correct this.

INSTRUCTIONS FOR ONE PERSON
Make a small bend in the last 5" (12 cm) of the came or ribbon. Grasp the straight end of the lead with pliers. Step on the bent end firmly with your heel, using all your weight. With all your strength, pull the lead until it stretches and continue until it feels stiff.

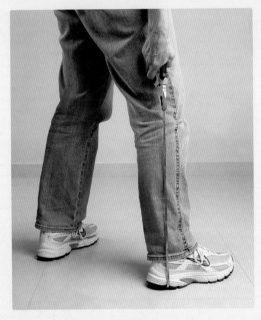

Squeeze the pliers firmly and pull straight up to avoid tearing the end of the came.

INSTRUCTIONS FOR TWO PEOPLE
Grasp each end with pliers. Step away from each other until the lead is straight between you. Pull until the lead stretches, and continue until it feels stiff and has no more give. Note that when two people stretch lead, it can tear suddenly, causing one or both people to fall back or tumble over. Before you start stretching lead, look behind you and make sure the area is free of glass, sharp objects, and hot tools.

Border the Panel with Lead Came

26. Stretch the *U* came. Cut off the bent sections at the ends by snipping the arms of the *U* and wiggling the end piece back and forth until it comes off.

27. Cut the stretched came into four pieces using the technique in Step 26. Two pieces should fit the long sides of the panel, and two should fit the short sides of the panel. With metal snips, trim the ends at a 45-degree angle. Throw out the cut lead scraps immediately.

28. Stand the panel on its side, over one of the longer pieces of came, with the corners aligned. Verify that the lead length matches the panel edge (if longer, trim). Press the panel gently downward while rocking the panel slightly to widen the came's channel where needed (such as around nuggets), and insert the panel into the came. When the panel can't be lowered anymore, and the panel is standing straight, the piece is ready to be tack-soldered.

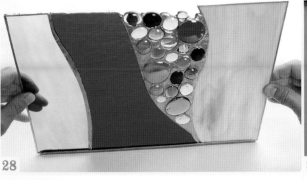

28

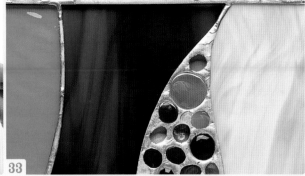

33

34

36

29. Hold the panel firmly with one hand. Without lifting the panel from the workboard, apply flux to the lead came where it meets copper or soldered seams, and to the unsoldered copper. Tack-solder by first wiping a bit of solder across the lead, then dabbing solder onto the copper or solder seam and wiping it quickly toward the lead. The soldered seams will meet and hold the came in place. While the solder must adhere to the lead came, it's important not to touch the lead with the soldering iron, which would melt the came. Let the tack solder cool.

30. Turn the panel so that the edge with the came is at the top. Set the second long piece of came on the workboard. Repeat Steps 28 and 29.

31. Turn the panel so that it rests on one of the short sides. Repeat Steps 28 and 29 using a short piece of stretched came. Tack-solder the lead came to the corner. Repeat for the last side of the panel.

32. Remove all the solder drips from the workboard before continuing—laying your panel on solder drips could cause it to crack.

33. Lay the panel on the table, face up. Apply flux to the copper seams and the came. Full-solder all the areas where the panel seams meet the came, working from inside the panel toward the came. When filling the space between the nuggets and the came border, place the damp soldering rag under the nuggets to catch the flowing solder. It isn't necessary to cover all the lead came with solder, only where it meets the panel seams.

34. Apply flux to the corners. Slide the damp soldering rag under a corner, pulling it up to cradle the panel. Solder the corners with a very light hand so as not to melt the lead came.

35. Turn the panel over. Following the techniques used for the first side of the panel, flux all tacked areas and full-solder.

36. Apply a layer of solder to the outside corner joint.

37. Check around the border and clean up any solder drips with the soldering iron by heating them and shaking them off, to the table, or by melting them into other soldered areas. Touch the came directly with the soldering iron as little as possible.

(Continued on next page)

39

40

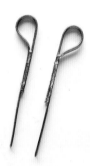

42

43

Add Hanging Loops

38. Stretch the lead ribbon. With the metal snips, cut the ribbon in half.

39. Lay the ribbon strips next to each other. Place a round object, such as the barrel of a fat marker, about two-thirds down the ribbon.

40. Fold the ribbon over the marker. Press the strips down together so that the loops are made the same shape and size. Remove the marker.

41. Turn the loops on the side. Apply flux to the lead. Pinch together and solder with a very light hand. Let cool.

42. Apply flux and solder the second side of the loops. Let cool. Trim the corners off the ends.

43. Lay the panel face up on the worktable. Lay the ruler along the top. Place the lead loops against the sides of the panel, when the tops of the loops meet the ruler. Apply flux. With a quick hand, solder the loops to the panel. Let cool. Turn the panel over and repeat, soldering the loops to the panel. Check the panel and clean up any solder drips. Let cool.

44. Wash the panel with dishwashing liquid and water. Dry well.

46

Add Shells (optional)

Shells are a fun inclusion, perhaps because they're so unexpected. Like all nonmetal items, they must be foiled and soldered before they can be added to your panel. The panel should be washed and dried before adding shells because it will be very hard to clean under shells after they're soldered into place. Patina and finishing compound should be applied after adding the shells.

45. Wash and dry two or three seashells.

46. Wrap a band of copper foil around the centerline of one of the shells. Press the foil to the shell's surface and burnish. Add a second wrap, overlapping the first, to better cup the shell. Burnish well.

47. Apply flux and coat the copper with solder. Wipe clean.

48. Rest the shell on the panel so that the solder on the shell touches a solder seam in the panel. It's best if the shell can be soldered to a seam in at least two places.

49. Without adding flux, solder the shell to the panel, wherever it touches a seam.

Finishing

50. Wash the panel. Dry well.

51. Check the panel to be sure it's dry; water tends to get trapped under the lead came. If you find water in the seams or borders, stand the panel over a towel in a safe place for twenty minutes so that any water trapped under the lead came can drain out. Dry again.

52. Put on latex gloves. With a cotton ball, apply patina to blacken all the panel seams, on both sides, and all the lead came, including the inside of the loops. Let sit for twenty to forty minutes.

53. Repeat Steps 50 and 51.

54. Apply finishing compound to all the seams and the lead came.

CHAPTER

4

Glass
Fusing

Fusing is a "warm" glass technique—it requires cold work (cutting), layering the cold glass, and application of intense heat in a kiln to bond the pieces. After the piece cools, we can use it in stained glass, display it as it is, or fire it again at a lower temperature to shape the piece into a mold.

Artists must take into account the physical properties of the glass they have chosen when preparing the design. Each fuse is quite lengthy to avoid stresses that might cause the piece to shatter during the fusing or afterward. Fusing results can be hard to predict or control; many fusers feel that the magic of fusing is in the moment that we open the kiln to discover what we have made.

TIP **Firing Schedules**

Fusing glass requires firing it in a kiln. To download the author's firing schedules, visit **www.glassandlight.blogspot.com**. You can also go to Quarry's website at **www.quarrybooks.com** and search for *The Glass Artist's Studio Handbook* and find a link to them there.

Fusing Glass

Regular art glass (the kind used for stained glass and mosaics) is not used in fusing; fusing glass is manufactured specifically for kiln work. The physical properties of the glass used in each design, notably its COE, determine how we program our kiln (see "Selecting Glass" for more information about COE). Manufacturers test their fusing glass for COE compatibility, strength, and how it behaves when fired. It's critical that each project use glass from only one COE family. Most fusing glass is sold in sheets. Additional types of fusing glass include frit and dichroic glass.

Fusing glass is specifically manufactured for work in a kiln. Small bits of shiny dichroic glass rest on sheet glass. Each color of frit has been ground to a different size.

FRIT

Frit for warm and hot work is made by grinding glass into small chunks or powder. Frit can be scattered onto glass before firing (a thin layer of glass glue will help it stay in place). Powders can be dusted onto glass glue or oil, or mixed with a material called Liquid Stringer, which is similar to thick glue. If you purchase frit by weight, ask the seller to mark the bag with the frit's color and COE and to note whether it's opaque or transparent. You won't remember those details when you want to use frit in your designs, and appearances can be deceiving because some glass *strikes*—changes color—in the kiln. When using glass frit, especially powder, wear a dust mask or filter to protect your lungs.

DICHROIC GLASS

Dichroic glass is a specialty glass made with a thin coat of metals on one surface. It's very pretty, with colors that shift in the light. Dichroic glass can be fused as is or *capped*—covered—with a layer of clear glass.

Other Materials
GLASS GLAZES

Common glass glazes are sold as powders. To prepare glaze, wear a dust mask or respiratory filter and put a spoonful of powdered glaze in a disposable cup. Add a few drops of fusing glue or oil to the powder and mix evenly. Add a few drops of water and mix some more; continue adding water until the glaze has a smooth, thin consistency. Use more oil when preparing a metallic glaze. Some artists use only oil when mixing gold glaze; 100 percent oil-based glaze requires about two weeks to dry, and all glaze must be dry before it can be kiln-fired or it will bubble, crack, or smear.

Glaze can be applied with a toothpick or a paintbrush. Test-fire glaze samples before using them in your work; some are better suited as underglazes and some work best at specific temperatures. If your design calls for two colors that touch, apply the first color and let it dry completely before you add the second color. In general, glass glazes are not COE-specific.

Mixing powder with water to make a glass glaze

FIBER PAPER

Fiber paper is manufactured in several thicknesses and is very useful because it's heat-resistant and won't burn in the kiln during a firing. Very thin fiber paper, also called kiln shelf paper, looks almost like ordinary typing paper. Thicker fiber paper can be cut into shapes and used to create bead holes or pockets in your work. Several layers of thick fiber paper can protect the bottom of your kiln, while fiberboard, a compressed sheet of the same material, can be cut or carved to create molds. (All of these uses will be covered in more detail later in this chapter.)

KILN WASH

Kiln wash is brushed onto items such as the kiln floor or molds to form a barrier; without it, hot glass would adhere to molds and kiln bricks. Kiln wash is sold as a powder. To make a batch of kiln wash, wear a dust mask or respiratory filter and put ½ cup of powder into a clean basin. Add 2 cups of water and mix well. Once the powder is dissolved into the water, you can remove the mask.

Fusing Kilns

The most important tool for fusing is a digitally controlled fusing kiln. Most commercial fusing kilns run on electricity and are made from firebrick blocks, electric spring coils, a pyrometer, a digital controller, and hardware. The coils run through the sides and the lid and radiate heat. The pyrometer measures the temperature inside the kiln and feeds this information back into the digital controller, which raises, lowers, or holds the temperature in the kiln. There are two common styles of digital controllers; instructions for programming them can be found in part 1. Selecting the right kiln for your needs requires some thought and is covered in detail in part 1. Kilns must be prepared before a firing—a process covered later in this chapter.

Ring by Aimee Mitchell. Fused glass set into a silver ring.

Basic Kiln Techniques

SLUMPING, TACKING, AND FULL FUSE

As glass heats, it softens before it melts. We can plan what will happen to our glass by controlling the rate of temperature change and the length of time we stay at specific temperatures. Three common fusing processes are full fuse, tacking, and slumping:

Full fuse: In a full fuse, layered glass is heated until the molecular bonds loosen throughout, melting the layers into one smooth piece, called a blank. Full fuse is the hottest kiln technique we will explore in the projects in this book.

Tack fuse/tacking: Tacked glass is heated until the molecular bonds on the surface of every piece loosen enough to bond the pieces together. If there are unsupported layers, they will sag and bond where they touch other glass. The resultant blank will clearly retain the shapes of the cut pieces used in the design. Tacking is a good technique to use when you want surface texture in your fused creation.

Slumping: Before glass gets hot enough to fuse, it will sag and stretch until it reaches a hard surface that can support it. Deliberately sagging glass is called *slumping.* The technique can be used to form bowls, plates, vases, and sculptures. In a complex piece, we first create a flat blank, then slump the blank into a mold.

PREPARING KILNS FOR FIRING

Before firing, the floor of the kiln must be protected from melting glass. This can be done with layers of thick fiber paper coated with kiln wash. The thickest fiber paper, on the bottom, can last for years. Moderately thick fiber paper, laid over the bottom layer, should be replaced every few firings when it starts breaking up. Top all the layers with several layers of kiln wash, brushed on in different directions. (Take care not to splash kiln wash on the electrical coils.) Fused pieces pick up the texture of whatever they're resting on during the firing. To create a very smooth surface, add a sheet of kiln shelf paper after the kiln wash has dried, and set the glass upon it. The kiln shelf paper will disintegrate during firing. After removing the glass from the kiln, put on a face mask or respiratory filter and clean out the powdery residue with a dustpan and brush. Apply kiln wash and a new layer of shelf paper. The kiln will be ready for its next firing.

PREPARING MOLDS FOR FIRING

With the kiln wash brush, apply several layers of kiln wash to all parts of your mold. When the wash has dried, use a piece of smooth paper to lightly burnish the wash and remove any brush marks or fingerprints.

To create the appearance of pieces next to each other but not touching, design your project with a large glass base, and fuse everything into it.

Basic Fusing Techniques

PREPARING GLASS

Techniques for cutting and grinding glass for fusing projects are identical to those used for stained glass (see "Cutting Glass"). It's essential that the glass be very clean before firing because adhesive or dirt will burn and distort or discolor your fired piece.

DESIGNING FOR FUSING

When moving from stained glass to fusing, our challenge is to think in layers. When glass heats, it first pulls in, then spreads. When it cools, it shrinks in again, and the overall size, shape, and thickness will be slightly altered. Pieces that are resting next to each other in the kiln, even if their edges are touching before firing, are not likely to fuse together properly; some overlap is needed.

TIP | **Design Tip: Fusing Colors**

When glass fuses, the colors don't mix. Opaque red and yellow don't become orange; they become one piece of glass with some red areas and some yellow areas, as one color pushes away or covers the other. Transparent colors layered over each other might give the appearance of blended colors.

The blue and orange patterns of the butterfly wings were created with two to four layers of glass.

Design Tip: Preparing Fusing Glass

When creating a fused element for a stained glass project, prepare all the fusing glass pieces at least ½" (1 cm) larger in every direction than needed for the stained glass pattern. If desired, use glaze to outline the pattern piece on the glass before firing. After firing, cut off the extra glass.

Designs can include many layers. It's very important to give each piece support from several places, or it might slide during firing. Place small pieces of clear glass under edges of pieces that are precariously balanced to support them. Complicated or delicately balanced pieces can be constructed right in the kiln.

PATTERNS FOR FUSING

When we create patterns for stained glass, we make one pattern and cut it into pieces. When designing complex fused pieces, we create several copies of a pattern and cut them up in different ways. By stacking the patterns before cutting even one piece of glass, we can consider how effectively our glass layers will overlap.

Special Techniques

MAKING MOLDS FROM FIBERBOARD

Also known as *Sera Board,* fiberboard is a fun material to use. It commonly comes in thin sheets (³/₈" or 1 cm thick) and can be cut, carved, and chiseled into whatever shape you need for your design. It can be layered to create molds with height, wells, and interesting shapes. If you layer fiberboard, don't undercut—that is, don't have a large piece balancing on a small piece—because the hot glass will fill the gap at the

Forming Bead Holes

Fused pendants and beads, such as the fused pendant project in this chapter, need a hole for the chain, lace, or wire on which they will be strung. Thick fiber paper (not kiln shelf paper) can easily be used for this purpose. You'll need scissors (pattern shears are best) and a 2" (5 cm) square of thick fiber paper.

TECHNIQUE:

1. With the scissors, cut a thin strip from the edge of the fiber paper. If you're using pattern shears, remove the thin strip of paper from between the scissor blades. If you're using regular scissors, cut very close to the edge.

2. Place the strip between the top and bottom layers of glass that you'll be fusing, exactly where you want the bead hole to be. Some of the strip should extend on both sides of the glass.

3. To support the top piece of glass, put small pieces of glass in the middle, on both sides of the fiber paper strip.

4. After firing, wash the fiber paper out of the hole.

ECO-TIP Egg Carton Driers

Do your eggs come in pressed-carton containers? If so, save the cartons for your studio! They're extremely absorbent and excellent for drying glass.

bottom and trap your mold inside. Fiberboard molds can be used repeatedly if treated well. They should be given a new coat of kiln wash before each use.

Fiberboard has the consistency of semi-hard cheese. Use a craft knife to cut or carve it. Don't try to cut through all the board at once. Start by scoring your pattern in the top. Continue sawing downward, a little at a time, until you cut all the way through. Store all the leftover pieces in an airtight bag for use in a future design.

All fiberboard molds must be coated with a layer of kiln wash before they can be used.

Safety Alert!

Fiberboard is an irritant. As you cut it, fibers are released and become airborne. Always wear latex gloves and a face mask or respiratory filter when working with fiberboard. The gloves and mask should stay on until you've cleaned up your work area using a damp cloth or wet paper towel.

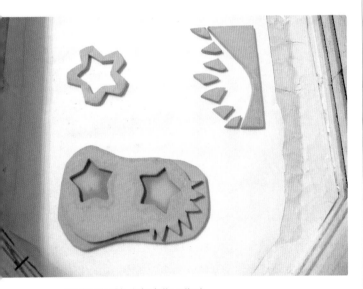

Fiberboard molds, drying in the author's kiln. The drier the kiln wash is, the lighter it appears. The molds can't be used until they're completely dry.

TIP Design Tip: Sizing Glass for Molds

To design a fused piece with depth, such as a bowl, first measure the diameter and dimensions of the mold you'll be using. Cut your base glass just a bit smaller on all sides than the top of the mold. Your first fuse will be either a tack fuse or a full fuse on the flat surface of the kiln floor to create a flat blank. Your second fuse will slump your blank into the mold.

This serving dish was made in two steps. In the first step, eleven pieces of glass were layered and painted with gold glaze, and fired to a full fuse. In the second step, the fused blank was slumped into a plaster mold. The mold's kiln wash coating bleached from pink to white from the kiln's heat.

Understanding and Correcting Common Fusing Mistakes

If we can be thrilled by the magic of fused glass when we open a kiln after a firing, it's likely that we might also occasionally be disappointed or perplexed. When things don't come out as expected, it's best to apply a little detective work so that we can either avoid or repeat the effect.

Sharp sides and points: If you fused pieces of glass without grinding them first, there may be little bits of glass left along the edges that could turn into sharp

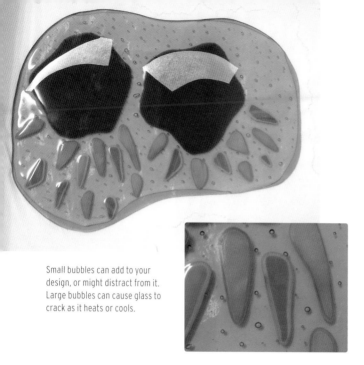

Small bubbles can add to your design, or might distract from it. Large bubbles can cause glass to crack as it heats or cools.

Cracks: Several types of cracks appear in glass, and each indicates a different problem. If the crack has smooth, melted edges, it occurred before your piece reached full fusing temperature and most likely indicates that the temperature of the kiln was raised too quickly. If the cracks have sharp, fresh edges, the piece cracked as it cooled. The annealing schedule might be off (not enough time, not the right temperature) or two or more pieces of glass with different COEs may have been combined. COE incompatibility can also cause part of your piece to shatter into slivers or crumble into small chunks. Sometimes purchased fusing glass is mislabeled, but most often COE compatibility issues occur when glass of one COE has been accidentally stored with glass of a different COE, leading us to unknowingly mix glass of different COE families within the same fused piece. If you suspect you have a COE compatibility issue, be extremely vigilant so that you can discover which glass is from a different COE group. Unfortunately, until you figure that out, everything you make will most likely crack either in the kiln or shortly afterward. An easily avoided cause of cracks is opening the kiln too soon; don't open a kiln after a firing until the digital controller reading indicates that the temperature inside has dropped below 170°F (76°C).

points. You might also have fired your kiln too hot. Grind your pieces and reduce your full fuse firing temperature by a few degrees and see if that prevents sharp sides and points.

Misplaced fuse: If a piece of glass fused in a different place than where you expected it to, it was not supported fully when it was set up in the kiln and most likely slid out of place before it tacked. Remember, thinner glass will slump faster than thick glass, and all glass slumps before it fuses. Next time, provide more support for the glass, unless you like the results and hope to repeat them. Support can be provided by stacking little bits of clear fusing glass under the edge of a larger top piece.

Bubbles: Bubbles appear in fused glass when air is trapped between the layers. This can be attractive, but if you want to prevent bubbles, before fusing two large sheets of glass together, place small squares of clear glass between the layers, every few inches (or centimeters). As the kiln heats, the clear glass will support the top layer long enough for the sandwiched air to exit at the sides before the edges melt together. If you find bubbles in small pieces of fused glass, either something on one of the layers or on the underside of the glass (adhesive from a sticker, for instance) burned during the fusing or the kiln wash was not dry before the kiln firing was started.

Raising the temperature of your kiln too quickly is one source of cracking. Cracks such as these are fatal; they can't be repaired.

Fused
FUSING PROJECT Pendant

Slip this easy-to-make pendant onto a leather lace or simple silver chain to dress up your t-shirt and sweater days. Charming, unique, and cheerful!

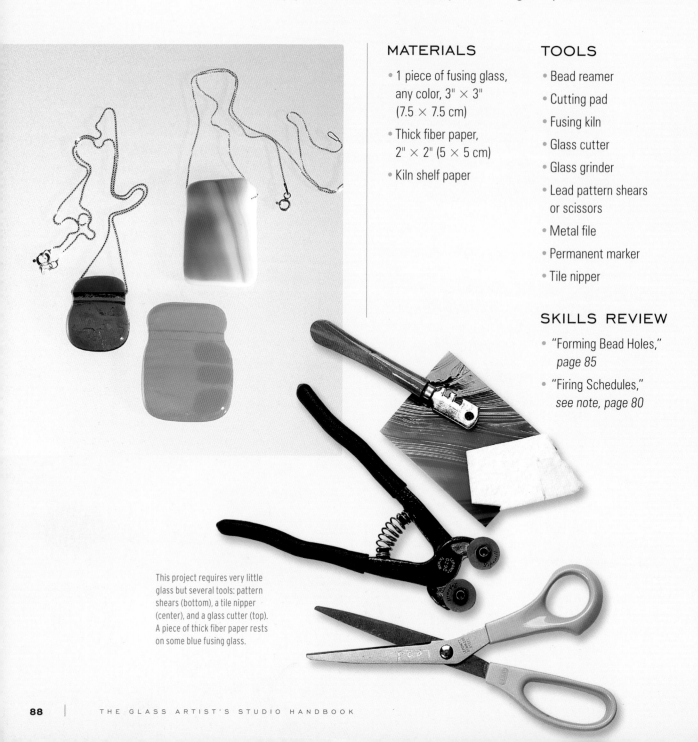

MATERIALS

- 1 piece of fusing glass, any color, 3" × 3" (7.5 × 7.5 cm)
- Thick fiber paper, 2" × 2" (5 × 5 cm)
- Kiln shelf paper

TOOLS

- Bead reamer
- Cutting pad
- Fusing kiln
- Glass cutter
- Glass grinder
- Lead pattern shears or scissors
- Metal file
- Permanent marker
- Tile nipper

SKILLS REVIEW

- "Forming Bead Holes," *page 85*
- "Firing Schedules," *see note, page 80*

This project requires very little glass but several tools: pattern shears (bottom), a tile nipper (center), and a glass cutter (top). A piece of thick fiber paper rests on some blue fusing glass.

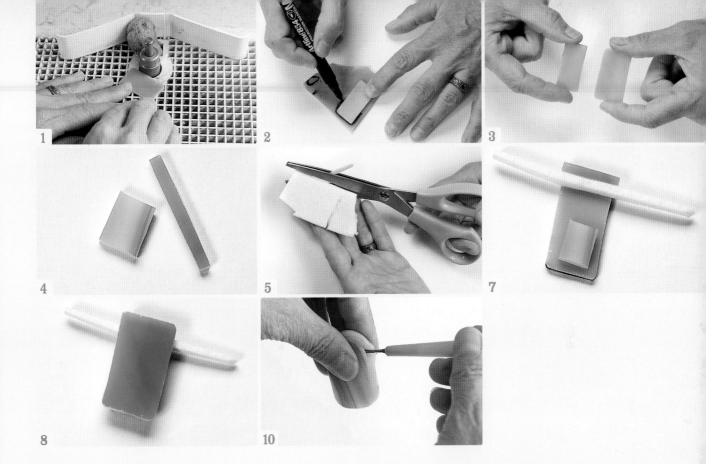

INSTRUCTIONS

1. Cut a 1" × 1.5" (2.5 × 4 cm) rectangle from the fusing glass. Grind the rectangle to round the corners. Wash with dishwashing liquid and water, and dry. This will be the back of the pendant.

2. Place the pendant back on the remaining fusing glass. With the marker, outline the pendant back.

3. Cut out the new rectangle along the outline. Grind the edges, rounding the corners. Wash with dishwashing liquid and water, and dry. This piece will be the pendant front. (It will be slightly larger than the pendant back.)

4. From the remaining glass, cut two glass supports: 1" × 1/8" (2.5 × 0.5 cm) and 1/2" × 1/2" (1 × 1 cm). Grind the pieces. Wash with dishwashing liquid and water, and dry.

5. Cut the thick fiber paper with the pattern shears. Carefully remove the thin strip of fiber paper from between the blades of the shears. If you don't have pattern shears, use scissors to cut a very thin strip of thick fiber paper. If the strip tears, discard and repeat this step.

6. Prepare the kiln for firing. Place the pendant back in the kiln on a piece of kiln shelf paper.

7. Place the thin glass support on the pendant back, aligning the top edges. Set the square glass support on the pendant back, toward the bottom. Place the strip of thick fiber paper on the pendant back, against the thin support. The fiber paper strip must extend beyond the pendant on both sides.

8. Cover all the pieces with the pendant front.

9. Fire full fuse with the schedule appropriate for the COE of your glass.

10. When the firing is complete, remove the pendant and wash off any residue. Wash the channel of fiber paper from the bead hole, using the bead reamer. File off any sharp edges, holding the glass underwater as you file.

Fused and Slumped
FUSING PROJECT Tea Light Dish

Enhance the romance in your life with this beautiful candleholder. The light of the flames will dance over the colors of the fused glass, while the tea light candles rest safely in a well.

MATERIALS

- 1 sheet of transparent colored fusing glass, any color, 8¼" × 5¼" (21 × 13.5 cm)
- 1 sheet of clear fusing glass, size 8" × 5" (20.5 × 12.5 cm)
- 2 pieces of fiberboard, 6" × 3" (15 × 7.5 cm), ³⁄₈" (1 cm) thick
- Assorted scraps of transparent and opaque colored fusing glass
- 2 tea light candles, each 1½" (4 cm) in diameter
- Kiln wash
- Kiln shelf paper

COE Alert: All the glass used must belong to the same COE family.

TOOLS

- Craft knife
- Cutting pad
- Disposable respiratory mask
- Fusing kiln
- Glass cutter
- Kiln wash brush
- Latex gloves
- Tile nipper

SKILLS REVIEW

- "Making Molds from Fiberboard," *page 85*
- "Kiln Wash," *page 83*
- "Firing Schedules," *see note, page 80*

Here is everything you need to complete this project. Although it has many steps, it isn't complicated.

INSTRUCTIONS

Prepare the Slumping Mold

1. Wearing the latex gloves and respiratory mask, use the craft knife to carve two 2¼" (5.5 cm) -diameter holes in one piece of fiberboard. With the craft knife, trim any rough edges. The holes should be evenly spaced across the length and width of the fiberboard.

2. Place the first piece of fiberboard (with the holes) on the second piece of fiberboard. The holes in the fiberboard correspond to where the tea lights will sit. This is your mold.

3. Coat each piece of fiberboard with kiln wash. Restack as before and leave to dry.

Prepare the Fused Blank

4. Place the sheet of clear (colorless) glass on kiln shelf paper in your kiln.

5. Place the sheet of transparent colored glass on the clear glass.

6. Decorate the rest of the surface of the glass sheet with the glass scraps. If you cut the scraps with the tile nipper or glass cutter, grind and wash them before adding them to the project.

7. Fire full fuse with the schedule appropriate for the COE of your glass.

8. When the firing is complete, remove the blank and wash off any residue with water.

Slump the Blank

9. Prepare the kiln for firing. Place the dry mold on kiln shelf paper in the kiln. Place the blank on the mold, with the mold centered under the blank and even margins all around.

10. Slump fire according to the appropriate firing schedule for your glass.

11. After the kiln has cooled, remove the dish. Wash to remove any residue, dry, and place tea lights in the wells.

CHAPTER
5

Lampworking

Lampworking, also called *flameworking,* is the craft and art of using fire to create beads, sculptures, and more from melted glass. You'll be working with a torch and an open flame, so this is definitely a "hot" glass technique! Glass beads have been made using this technique for a very long time. In fact, glass beads were used as currency in several parts of the world hundreds of years ago. Recent technical developments, particularly in torches and lampworking kilns, give us more control and (when done correctly) make our beads stronger.

TIP	**Annealing Schedules**

Annealing beads is best done in a lampworking kiln. To download the author's annealing schedules, visit **www.glassandlight.blogspot.com**. You can also go to Quarry's website at **www.quarrybooks.com** and search for *The Glass Artist's Studio Handbook* and find a link to them there.

As you learn this technique, you'll have fun, and probably create some funny-looking beads at first. Save these—they'll be proof of your progress as you improve with practice, and will be useful for making beaded accents and decorating hanging wires on suncatchers.

At the torch, you'll work equally with both hands, but you might find that some activities are easier with your dominant hand. Note that your tools, glass, and safety equipment should always be placed within reach of your dominant hand so that you don't have to reach around the flame to pick them up.

Selecting Glass: Soft vs. Hard

Glass for lampworking is sold in long, pencil-thin rods (sometimes called *canes*). *Hard glass* usually refers to borosilicate glass. Borosilicate glass, also known as *boro,* has a COE of 33 (see "Selecting Glass" in part 2 for more about COE and its significance in hot and warm glass work). *Soft glass* refers to glass families with COEs of 90, 96, and 104—the higher the COE, the softer the glass.

Many people prefer COE 104 for lampworking because it's generally cheaper and more readily available. COE 104 melts quickly and can be used with a simple torch such as a Hot Head. I prefer COE 96 glass when working with soft glass, and boro for its magnificent, unpredictable color shifts. While I don't recommend boro to beginners, any of the soft glasses will do as a starting point.

If you wish to experiment with more than one glass family, take extra care to store the different COEs separately and to label them clearly with their COE so as never to mix them. Remember: It's impossible to identify the COE of a glass rod by visual inspection.

In the most popular lampworking style, the flame-worker wraps the hot glass around thin metal sticks called mandrels. When the bead cools, the mandrel is removed, leaving a hole running through the glass. It's fairly simple to make a basic bead if you have the right equipment.

Before You Light the Torch

Many beginners are confounded at first by the coordination required to make a bead in the flame, as they sit directly behind a large flame, grasping a glass rod in one hand and a mandrel in the other. To heat the rod, you'll poke it in and out of the center of the flame; at the same time, you'll spin the mandrel at the far tip of the flame. It's like patting your head while rubbing your tummy with a circular motion. Once you have wound glass onto the mandrel, you must continue to spin it or the hot glass will change shape and, perhaps, drip off. Drips are frustrating and potentially dangerous, depending on what they drip onto. Practicing your spin before lighting the torch is an excellent idea.

Practice the Spin

TECHNIQUE:

1. Grasp a mandrel so that most of the mandrel extends beyond your fingers. Form a supportive cradle with your first three fingers.

2. Use your forefinger and thumb to roll the mandrel away from you by pulling your thumb up while pushing your forefinger down.

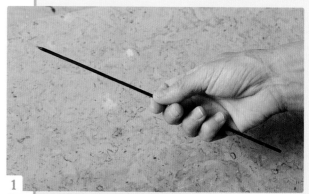

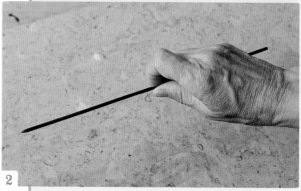

It doesn't matter which hand you practice with first; you'll need to practice the spin with both hands. Aim to keep the mandrel as steadily horizontal as possible while keeping the roll as smooth as you're able. If your mandrel jerks or tilts while spinning, you'll find it difficult to create an evenly shaped bead. Once you can spin a mandrel for several minutes with each hand, you're ready to start.

Dip at least 2" (5 cm) of mandrel into the bead release.

The author prefers a short plastic container with a wide base and a screw top for storing her bead release, as it's less likely to tip, spill, or dry out.

ABOUT MANDRELS

If you wrap hot glass on a mandrel without a protective coating, the glass will bond to the metal and you'll have to break your bead to remove it. Avoid this by coating one end of the mandrel—the working end, where you'll make your bead—with bead release, a ceramic compound that can be purchased as powder or as a premixed slush.

DIPPING MANDRELS

The materials in bead release separate over time; stir or shake your bead release until it's smooth and creamy again before dipping any mandrels in it. To coat the mandrel's end, slowly dip the mandrel into the jar of bead release and then set it to dry, with the dipped end at the top, in a can filled with sand, in a sponge, or in the top grid of your glass grinder.

Read the instructions on the bottle of bead release to learn whether yours must be completely dry before you can start making beads or whether you can quickly dry it in the flame as part of the lampworking process. If you're using homemade bead release, you'll need to experiment. I make my own bead release from kiln wash powder; I dip my mandrels at least one hour before I use them. Dip as many mandrels as you expect to work with in one lampworking session.

> **TIP** | **Bead Release Recipe**
>
> Make your own bead release with my secret recipe: 2 cups Bullseye Shelf Primer powder + ½ cup water. Wear a respiratory mask or filter while measuring the powder and adding the water. Stir with a long-handled spoon until the mix is creamy, about the consistency of thin cake batter. If you purchased a powdered bead release mix, add water as per the instructions on the packet. Make more than you'll need; if you close your jar well, your bead release should last a very long time. If it starts to thicken, it will be easy to add a little water and stir, stir, stir.

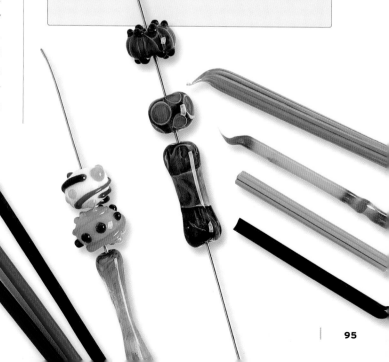

Soft glass (left) has stable colors. The colors in hard glass (right) shift and change when bathed in high concentrations of gas or oxygen. Although the soft and hard glass rods in this photo appear very different, in many cases it isn't possible to distinguish between them, so be sure to store them separately and label them clearly.

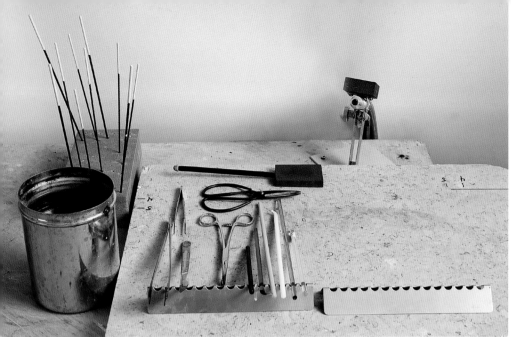

This photograph was taken facing the torch station. The lampworker will sit behind the torch, facing the camera. The table is topped with a marble slab. This station is set up for a right-handed person. The torch is a small bench burner fueled by an oxygen and gas mix.

A Hot Head torch screwed into a fuel canister. *Photo courtesy of Hot Head Source.*

SET UP YOUR TORCH TABLE

Lay your materials out on your workstation before lighting the torch: Place a rod rest on your heatproof tabletop, and position your glass on it. Place tools to your right if you're right-handed. If you'll be using frit, pour some in a small metal tray or onto a marver. Place an open jar or canister filled with water in the upper corner, where you can drop in hot glass or mandrels if you make a mess of them.

If you don't have a kiln and are planning to use vermiculite to cool your beads, place a metal can filled with clean vermiculite where you can reach it but where it won't be in your way. If you plan to cool your beads between pieces of fiber blanket, you can put these on the table, stacked. Put on your Ace or didymium lampworking safety glasses. Make sure nothing combustible is in the area of the projected torch flame or on the floor around the table. Turn on your ventilation system.

Lighting the Torch

LIGHTING A HOT HEAD TORCH

1. Remove the seal from the disposable fuel canister.
2. Screw the torch head firmly into the canister's neck, all the way down.
3. Secure the holder to the table with screws or a strong clamp.
4. Set the canister with the torch head into its holder so that it stands upright.
5. Click the BBQ lighter to get a small flame and hold it steady under the torch head, against the edge of the brass torch opening.
6. Quickly open the gas valve until a lot of gas is hissing from the torch.
7. Lift the BBQ flame into the line of the gas from underneath, very close to the bottom lip of the torch head, until the gas ignites.
8. Use the knob to turn the flame down as much as you can without extinguishing it.

LIGHTING A GAS AND OXYGEN TORCH

If your equipment includes a bench burner, use the popular P-O-O-P rule to light and extinguish your torch. When lighting your torch the order is P-O; first propane, then oxygen. (When extinguishing your torch the order to close the torch knobs is O-P.) This rule will hold true even if your gas of choice is not propane—light the gas first, and extinguish it last.

1. Verify that all torch knobs are *closed* and verify that your gas and oxygen sources are *open*. If you're using an oxygen concentrator, turn it on.
2. Click the BBQ lighter to get a small flame and hold it steady.
3. Twist the gas knob on the torch about one-half turn to open a small supply of gas and move the BBQ flame into the line of gas to light the flame.
4. Adjust the flame by adding or reducing the gas flow until the flame is about 6" (15 cm) long.
5. Slowly twist the oxygen knob on the torch to add oxygen to the flame.
6. Adjust the flame by adding or reducing gas until you have a soft, neutral flame. If your flame is bushy, lower the gas level a bit. If your flame is thin and very pointed, lower the oxygen level and add more gas.

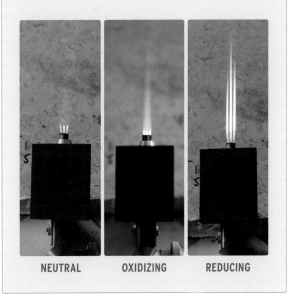

TIP | Name That Flame

Torch flames are named by the ratio of oxygen to gas. A neutral flame is balanced. An *oxidizing* flame has more oxygen than gas, and the flame will be narrow and pointed. A reducing flame has less oxygen and will be large and bushy. The colors and metals in boro glass and in some soft glasses are coaxed out and altered when the glass is bathed in an oxidizing or reducing flame, but most soft glass should be worked in a neutral flame.

NEUTRAL   **OXIDIZING**   **REDUCING**

Extinguishing the Torch

If you're working with a Hot Head, extinguish the flame by twisting the knob on the torch head with your fingers until it's firmly closed.

If you're working with a gas and oxygen torch, close the oxygen knob first and the gas knob second (O-P), and the source tanks (or gas tank and concentrator) last. Everything should be firmly closed and tightened only with your fingers. After closing the source tanks, it's a good idea to open the torch knobs again to release any leftover gas or oxygen in the hoses. If you do this, don't forget to close the knobs again after a minute or two.

Tricks of the Trade

Here are some hot tips to keep in mind as you work:

Heating the glass rod: Don't introduce the glass to the flame all at once. The sudden and extreme heat will cause the glass to shatter. Start at the end of the flame, as far as you can comfortably reach. Dip or poke the last 1" to 2" (2.5 to 5 cm) of the rod into the flame for a few seconds. After you've done that several times, the glass will start to glow with heat. When it's glowing, bring it into the center of the flame.

> **TIP**
>
> ## Building a Neutral Flame with an O₂ Concentrator
>
> If you're using an O_2 concentrator for your oxygen supply instead of a cylinder of concentrated oxygen, you won't have a preadjusted regulator. Instead, when you open your O_2 knob on the torch, keep an eye on the pressure indicator on your concentrator (see part 1, chapter 2, "Lampworking Torches," "Associated Hardware," for more information about concentrators). I open the O_2 knob on my torch until my concentrator shows 4.5. At that point, I leave the O_2 knob and adjust the flame by changing the flow of propane by fiddling with the gas knob.

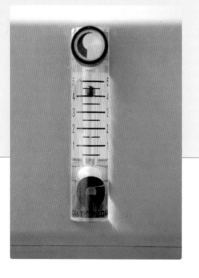

TOP The glow at the tip of the rod is a sign that the glass is very hot and soft.

ABOVE The glass rod will melt fastest in the center of the flame, but the mandrel should be warmed at the end of the flame.

Heating the mandrel: While you're heating the glass, you'll need to heat the mandrel as well; otherwise, the glass won't stick to the bead release. You can do this by waving it in and out toward the end of the flame, or by spinning it in the flame. If the bead release cracks, put the mandrel in your canister of water and start again with a new mandrel; this time, heat your mandrel slower and farther from the center of the flame.

Heat mapping: Heat mapping refers to being aware of the heat in your bead. With practice, you'll notice that as the bead cools, it changes color. Once you've heated the glass and started making a bead, you'll need to keep the bead fairly hot and evenly heated all the time. If one side of the bead cools and the other stays hot, your bead is likely to break. One way of controlling the heat in your bead is to spin the bead in the flame all the time, even when you're looking for another piece of glass, a tool, or a tray of frit. In this case, the temperature of the glass is controlled by its location in the flame. Another way is to occasionally reheat the entire bead at the very tip of the torch flame until the bead has an even glow on all sides. This is called *flashing*.

Cooling your bead: I always recommend kiln annealing to cool beads. But no matter what your method, the trick is to know *when* to put your bead in the kiln, in vermiculite, or between the layers of fiber blanket. Do this too soon and your bead will droop, pick up bits of vermiculite or blanket, or take the pattern of the bottom of the kiln. Wait too long and the glass will break. When you remove the bead from the flame, keep it spinning as the glow starts to fade. It's still very hot, so don't attempt to touch it or put it down. As the glow fades, you'll be able to see whether the heat is even or not—the cooler areas will be darker. If the bead glow isn't all the same color, flash the bead to reheat it evenly. Once you're sure that the bead is evenly heated, remove it from the flame altogether. As you spin the mandrel, count; sometime between twenty and thirty, your bead will lose its glow and the color will darken. This is the moment to put the bead in the kiln, bury it in vermiculite, or lay it between the fiber blankets. The glass is still well over 950°F (500°C) but should be hard enough not to change shape or stick to anything. The bead will cool on the mandrel.

Cleaning beads: Once the kiln chamber has cooled to almost-room temperature (less than 149°F or 65°C), you can retrieve the beads from the kiln. They might still feel quite hot to the touch, but they will cool rapidly in the open air. (If you're using another cooling method, leave the beads to cool overnight.) Place the mandrels in a basin or cup, with the bead end of the mandrel in the water, and let them soak for a while. To remove a bead from the mandrel, grasp the mandrel with a pair of pliers in one hand and twist the bead off with the other. If the bead doesn't come off the mandrel, try grasping the bead with cloth or a wet paper towel as you twist. After removing beads from mandrels, use a bead reamer to remove all traces of bead release from the bead hole, and then leave the beads to dry. Beads should be reamed under water.

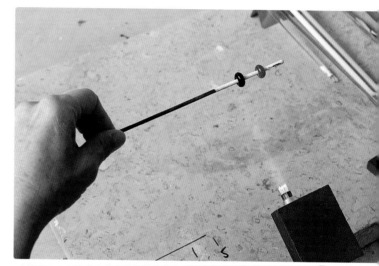

TOP Both beads were made from the same glass; the bead on the right is hotter than the bead on the left.

ABOVE Hold the mandrel firmly and twist the bead back and forth with very small movements until you've broken the baked bead release under the bead.

Dealing with the Unexpected

The lampworking process is less controlled than other techniques, and surprises abound. The following tips will help you make beautiful beads:

Colors aren't discernible: As you heat the glass, it will begin to glow. By the time it's hot enough to work with, the glass will glow red with heat and the original color will be difficult, or even impossible, to discern. If it's an opaque glass, it may appear transparent. If you're making a bead with several colors, lay the rods on the rod rest in the order you intend to use them, and put them back in the same order. If, when you're adding a new color, you can't see where you put the last one, swing the bead into the flame for a moment and the design should come up enough for you to distinguish the location of stripes and dots, even if you can't see what colors they are.

Glass doesn't stick: For the glass to stick to the mandrel, both must be hot. If, when you start making a bead, the glass doesn't stick to the mandrel, simply heat them up some more and try again.

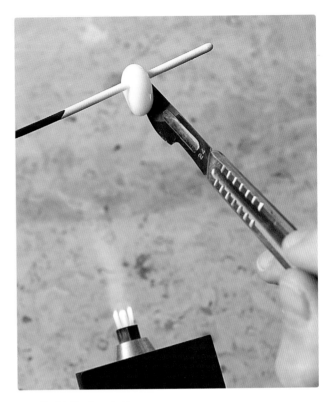

The flat side of a scalpel is convenient for straightening wilted beads.

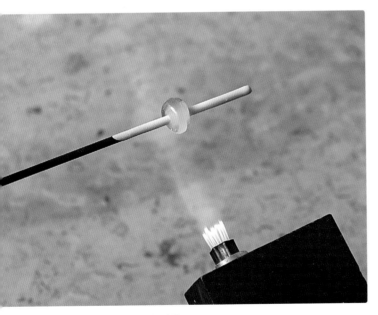

Look closely at this hot bead: It's decorated with a green strip over a white base. When the glass is glowing, the colors can't be identified, and must be remembered.

Bead slides on the mandrel: Sometimes the bead will break free and slide or slip on the mandrel. This happens when the bead release on the mandrel breaks off. Don't try to work on a bead like this—it can suddenly slide onto your hand or drop off the mandrel onto your clothes! Carefully put the bead in the kiln right away, or drop it into a water canister and let it shatter. To prevent your beads from coming loose, don't overheat the bead release and keep your glass hot. When winding glass, the rod must be very hot so that you can pull it away without tugging on the bead.

Glass is wilting: Particularly when making disks, glass can lose its shape and wilt. Remove it from the flame. While it's still hot, use a scalpel or the edge of a marver to gently move the glass back in line. If a round bead sags out of shape, remove it from the flame while continuing to spin it. Keep the areas with extra glass toward the top a bit longer as you spin, and gravity will help tug it down as the glass cools.

Bead won't come off the mandrel: Here are some tricks for getting a stubborn bead off a mandrel:

• Push the bead up and down on the mandrel instead of twisting back and forth.

• Wash all the bead release off the mandrel and leave the mandrel to soak for two to four days; occasionally attempt to twist it off with very small movements (the water loosens the hidden bead release).

• Put the whole thing in the freezer for a day (this contracts the metal and the glass and might separate them). Follow with another soak, if needed.

Glass bonded to the mandrel: Sometimes the bead bonds to the mandrel and can't be removed. If you really love the bead and want to keep it, clean the mandrel and stand it in a flowerpot or decorative bottle. If you want to be able to use the mandrel again and are willing to sacrifice the bead, the next time you turn on the torch slowly and carefully introduce the bead into the flame. When the glass is hot and the mandrel is red-hot, plunge them into a canister of water. The bead should shatter and break off. Reheat the mandrel and plunge it in the water again to remove any stray glass bits that might still be stuck to the metal.

Air bubbles trapped in the bead: If you work too close to the flame, the glass will overheat and boil. Its appearance will be white-hot rather than glowing red. This can happen on the rod or on the bead. Sometimes this leaves bubbles in the bead or a rough surface. If you see the glass boiling, work farther down the flame.

Decorations are breaking off: When you add dots and ribbons to beads, they must be heated enough to have a smooth, melted join to the bead or they'll break off after the bead cools. If you find it difficult to melt dots enough but not too much, work at the end of the flame where it's cooler and you'll have more control.

Bead has cracked: As with fusing, different cracks mean different things. If the bead cracks as you're making it, you've let it get too cool. If a bead leaves the kiln with cracks, you may not have flashed the bead enough, and the bead might have cooled unevenly. If the bead has a section that looks shattered inside, it's often a compatibility issue—either you've mixed glasses with different COEs or you've tried to include a noncompatible nonglass material. It's also possible that your annealing schedule was not correct; check the schedule to be sure you entered it correctly.

ECO·TIP | **Fruit Basket Bead Nets**

Plastic fruit baskets can be useful in a lampworking studio. If you're conserving water with a basin in the sink, the water will sometimes be murky. Drop a fruit basket into the basin water. As you remove beads from mandrels, drop them into the fruit basket. After the beads soak and you're ready to clean out the bead separator, it will be easy (and safer) to lift the basket out and retrieve your beads rather than fishing around the bottom of the basin with your fingers.

The author experimented with rolling beads in iron oxide powders; unfortunately, the iron oxide did not cool at the same rate as the glass, and the inside of the bead shattered.

Making a
LAMPWORKING PROJECT
Basic Bead

MATERIALS

• 1 glass rod, any color

TOOLS

• BBQ lighter
• Lampworking kiln or vermiculite or 2 pieces of fiber blanket
• Lampworking safety glasses
• Mandrels, dipped in bead release
• Rod rest
• Torch

INSTRUCTIONS

1. Set up your work area.

2. If you'll be using a kiln to anneal your beads, program it with the schedule appropriate for your glass and start it.

3. Put on safety glasses and light the torch.

4. With one hand, poke the glass rod into the flame several times to gradually heat it. With your other hand, spin or wave the mandrel in the end of the flame to preheat the bead release and mandrel. When the glass starts to change color and soften from the heat, bring the mandrel into the center of the flame.

Basic Bead Shapes

When glass is hot, it can be shaped with gravity or against a marver. These are some common bead shapes.

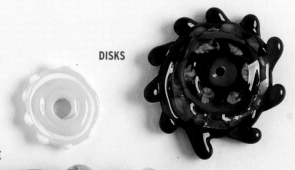

DISKS

BARREL, SPACERS, AND CONE

PRESSED TAB, BICONE, CUBE, AND TUBE

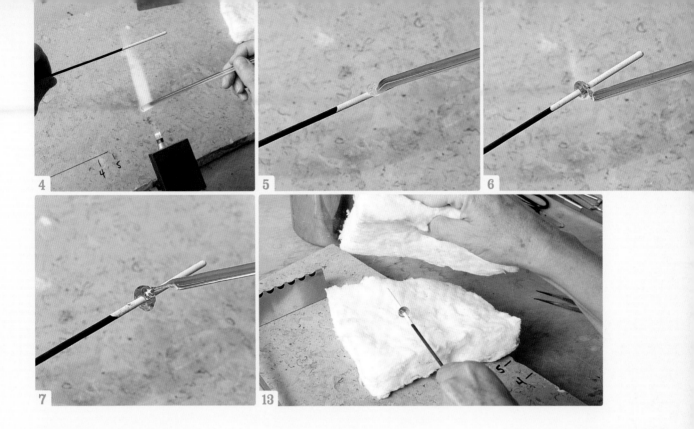

5. Touch the end of the glass rod to the mandrel and spin the mandrel away from you, winding soft glass onto the mandrel.

6. Keep spinning the mandrel away from you until the glass starts to cool. Move the end of the rod, above the bead, into the flame.

7. Pull the softened glass as you melt it until it separates from the bead as you spin the mandrel. Don't tug at the glass; let the flame melt through it.

8. If you wish to make a bigger bead, spin the bead just out of the flame until it cools a little, while reheating the end of the glass rod.

9. Repeat Steps 5–8 to add more layers to the bead until it's the desired size. (I recommend three to five wraps.)

10. Place the glass rod on the rod rest with the hot end away from you.

11. Continue spinning the mandrel in the flame until the glass softens, all layers melt, and the bead evens in shape.

12. While spinning the mandrel, remove it from the flame. Keep spinning the mandrel until the bead loses its color.

13. When the bead cools and darkens, place it in the kiln, in the vermiculite, or between the fiber blankets.

14. Repeat from Step 5–13 until you've used all your mandrels.

15. Extinguish the torch.

16. If you're using a lampworking kiln to anneal your beads, approach the digital control and manually Skip the annealing program to Step 2 to begin the annealing process.

Decorative Techniques

LAMPWORKING PROJECT

Glass can be decorated by adding more glass and either melting it in or leaving it raised against the bead. We sculpt beads by pressing them against textured metal, catching them in presses, twisting, poking, and pulling them, and cutting them with glass shears, to name but a few techniques. Use your imagination and don't be afraid to experiment!

MATERIALS

- 2 glass rods in contrasting colors
- At least 1 tablespoon of frit in a different color than the rods

TOOLS

- BBQ lighter
- Lampworking kiln or vermiculite or 2 pieces of fiber blanket
- Lampworking safety glasses
- Mandrels, dipped in bead release
- Metal frit tray
- Rod rest
- Torch

INSTRUCTIONS

Decorating a Bead with Frit

1. Place a bit of frit in a shallow metal tray.

2. Make a basic bead. When it's moderately glowing, roll it in the frit tray.

3. Some frit should stick to the bead's surface (if it doesn't, the bead isn't hot enough).

4. Melt the frit into the bead. Spin the bead until it starts to cool and place it in the kiln, the fiber blanket, or the vermiculite.

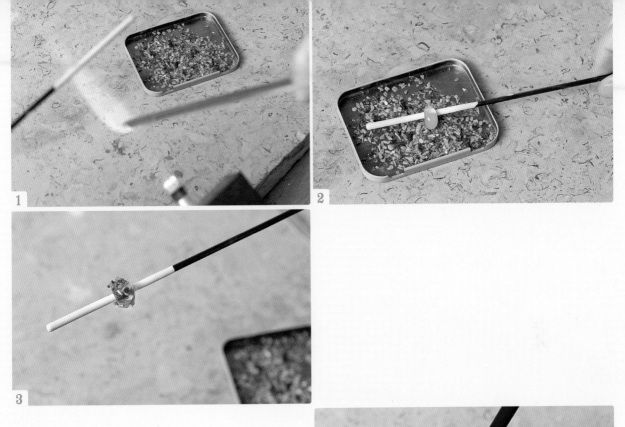

Adding Dots to a Bead

A popular way of decorating beads is to add dots. Dots can be stacked, layered, poked, and pulled, melted into the bead, and mashed. You can add as many rows of dots as you wish as long as each is melted enough to have a smooth connection to the bead's surface.

5. Decide what color glass you'll use for your base bead and what color you'll use for your dots.

6. Make a basic bead. When it's shaped, pull it from the flame and let it cool a bit as you spin the mandrel. The bead should cool enough so that it holds its shape even when not spinning.

7. Start heating the rod from another color.

8. Press the hot end of the rod against the bead, straight from the top.

9. Pull the rod up and away, without tugging on the bead.

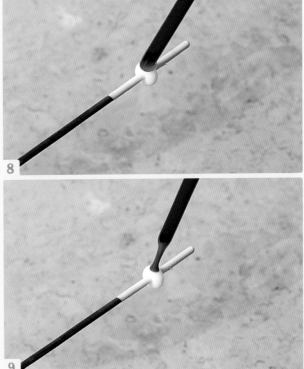

(Continued on next page)

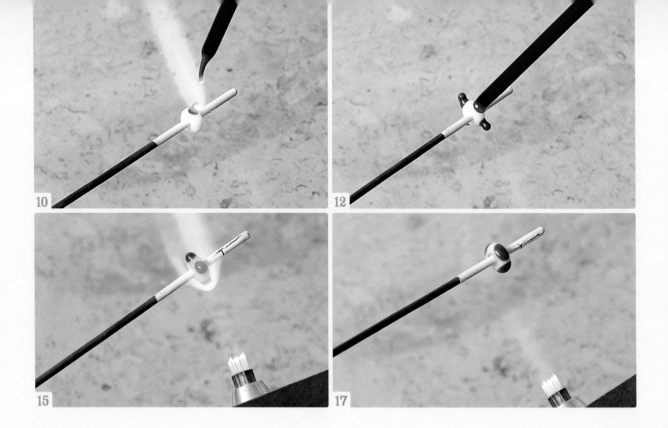

10. Use the flame to cut the strand of glass by melting through it.

11. Reheat the rod and turn the bead one half turn so that the dot is at the bottom. Repeat Steps 8–10.

12. Reheat the rod and turn the bead a quarter turn so that the dots are facing left and right. Repeat Steps 8–10.

13. Reheat the rod and turn the bead one half turn so that the area without a dot is at the top. Repeat Steps 8–10.

14. Set the rod down.

15. Spin the bead in the flame just enough to melt the edges of the dot smoothly to the bead.

16. If you wish to leave the dots raised, remove the bead from the flame and spin until the bead cools. Place it in a kiln, in vermiculite, or in fiber blanket.

17. If you wish to melt the dots into the bead, return the bead to the flame and continue heating it until the dots are smoothly melted into the bead's surface before placing the bead in a kiln, in vermiculite, or between layers of fiber blanket.

Disks and Hollow Beads

MATERIALS

- Glass rods in any color

TOOLS

- BBQ lighter
- Lampworking kiln or vermiculite or 2 pieces of fiber blanket
- Lampworking safety glasses
- Mandrels, dipped in bead release
- Rod rest
- Torch

Making a Disk Bead

Disks are beads with many layers. Each layer must be heated enough to bond to the layer below, but not enough to melt into it. As you stack the layers, the disk will grow in diameter, while staying thin, like a bicycle tire. Flash your bead often to keep it from cracking as you work. Don't keep it in the flame too long or the edges will wilt.

Making a Hollow Bead

Hollow beads are formed by creating two disks on one mandrel, with about ½" (1 cm) between them. By applying glass alternately to each side, both disks stay warm and are less likely to crack. After a few layers, the glass is layered toward the space between the disks, bringing them closer until they touch. When the disks are sealed against each other, and all small holes are closed, the hot air between the disks will help shape the hollow bead from the inside.

(Continued on next page)

A collection of disk beads and buttons. A disk's shape generously lends itself to personal expression.

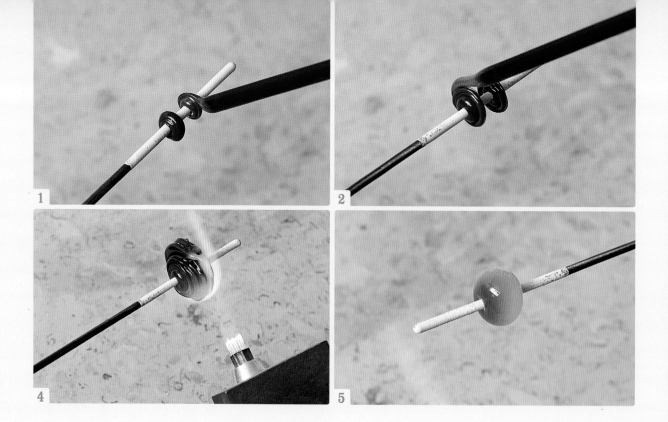

INSTRUCTIONS

1. Start two disks on the same mandrel, moving from one disk to the next as you add layers.

2. The first few layers should be layered straight up. After that, layer the glass toward the center, still alternating between sides.

3. When the disks get close enough, they'll touch. Flash the bead long enough to heat it evenly.

4. Heat the seam between the disks to melt and seal it. If you see holes in the disk walls, heat them briefly to close them. If the holes are large, patch them with hot glass.

5. Heat the bead in the flame. The air inside will expand and even out the bead as you spin the mandrel.

6. When the bead has the form that you want, remove it from the flame and keep spinning until it's cool.

7. If the bead loses its shape, return it to the flame and repeat Steps 5 and 6.

8. Place in a kiln, in vermiculite, or between layers of fiber blanket.

Annealing and Batch Annealing

Whenever possible, beads should be put into a hot lampworking kiln as they are made, and annealed immediately afterwards. If you don't have a lampworking kiln but do have a fusing kiln, it's possible to cool beads in vermiculite or between layers of fiber blanket and to anneal the beads later. This is called batch annealing. For safety's sake, all the mandrels must be removed before annealing beads in a fusing kiln. Most fusing kilns can anneal large quantities of beads. Because the beads are starting the annealing process at room temperature rather than hot from the flame, the kiln must be heated slowly to avoid shocking the glass.

SET UP THE KILN

Lampworking kilns do not require special preparations before using them. Program the kiln with the schedule appropriate for your glass and turn it on before lighting your torch. To set up a fusing kiln for batch annealing:

1. Remove all the beads from the mandrels. Set the mandrels aside.
2. Line the kiln floor with a piece of kiln shelf paper.
3. Place the beads on the shelf paper.
4. Close the kiln and turn on the digital programmer.

An assortment of hollow beads, decorated with dots and ribbons.

ALTERING A SCHEDULE FOR BATCH ANNEALING IN A FUSING KILN

5. Select the bead annealing schedule appropriate for your glass.
6. Alter the first step of the schedule as follows:
   a. Change the first rate from FULL to raising the kiln to the target temperature over two hours. (If your kiln measures Rate as the number of minutes to reach the target temperature, this will be Rm120. If your kiln measures Rate as the number of degrees to rise in one hour, Rd will equal one-half of your target temperature.)
   b. Change the first Hold to one minute.
7. Start the kiln.

TIP | Annealing Schedules

To download the author's annealing schedules, visit **www.glassandlight.blogspot.com**. You can also go to Quarry's website at **www.quarrybooks.com** and search for *The Glass Artist's Studio Handbook*. Most glass artists think of annealing schedules as flexible schedules that are altered over time according to the results they receive. You can change them if your experience shows that your kiln needs a different schedule.

Melding Skills
and Techniques:
Studio
Projects

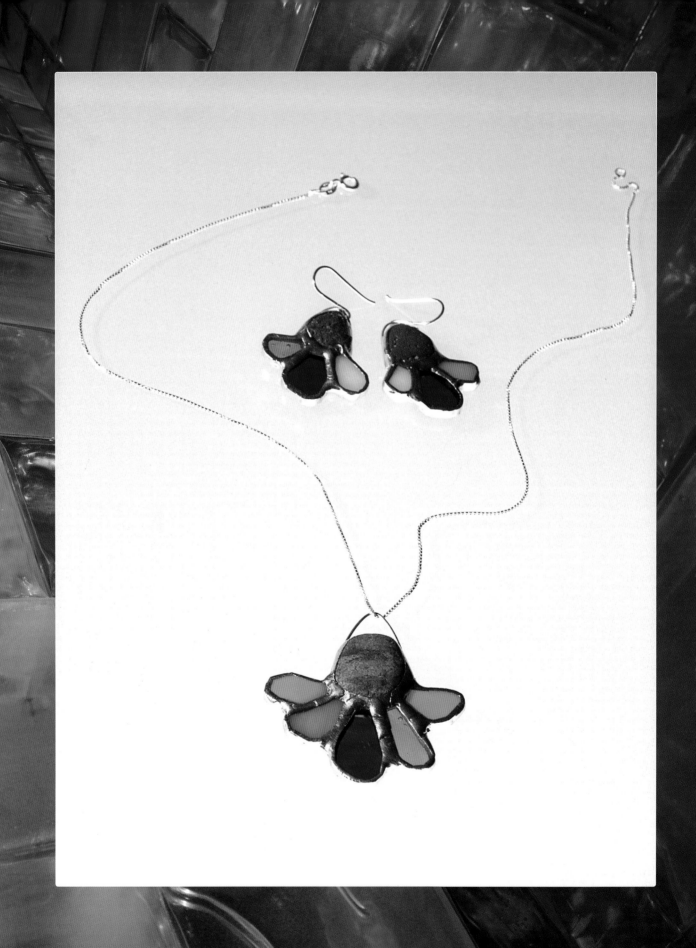

Stained Glass Pendant and Earring Set:

STUDIO PROJECT
Wild Roses

Make unique and eye-catching miniature stained glass flower jewelry with your art glass scraps, treasures from nature, and some purchased jewelry findings. The thin copper foil will give your creations a light, delicate look, and using lead-free solder will ensure that your jewelry will be safe to wear on your skin.

MATERIALS

- Several pieces of scrap glass, any color
- 3 similar centerpieces, each ¼" to ½" (6 mm to 1.3 cm) in diameter (polished rocks, flat sea or river pebbles, chandelier crystals, wood, etc.)
- Copper foil, ³/₁₆" wide
- Lead-free solder
- Flux
- Finishing compound
- Silver wire (sterling or plated), 18 or 20 gauge, 10" (25.5 cm)
- Purchased earring hooks
- Purchased chain
- Cotton balls

TOOLS

- Brass brush
- Burnisher
- Flux brush
- Grinder
- Pliers
- Soldering iron
- Tile nipper
- Wire cutter/metal snips

SKILLS REVIEW

- "Making Flower Petals with a Tile Nipper," *page 49*
- "Common Stained Glass Processes," *page 50*
- "More Than Glass," *page 56*
- "Using Lead-Free Solder," *page 55*

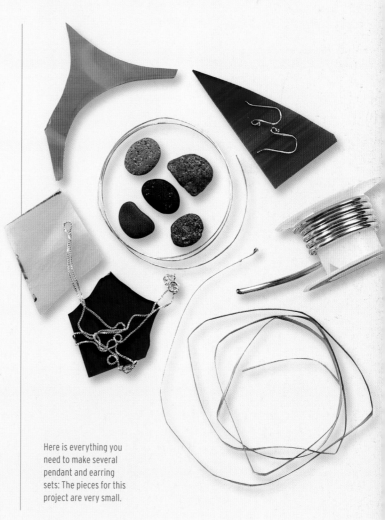

Here is everything you need to make several pendant and earring sets: The pieces for this project are very small.

INSTRUCTIONS

Prepare the Components

1. Clean the centerpieces by scrubbing them with a toothbrush, dishwashing liquid, and water. Dry well.

2. Wrap the centerpieces in copper foil. Burnish, and set aside.

3. With the tile nipper, break the glass scraps into small pieces. Trim each to an approximate petal shape about ½" (1.3 cm) long and ¼" (0.75 cm) wide at its widest point. It's best to prepare more petals than you'll need for your project.

4. Grind the edges of the petals, smoothing any sharp points. Wash and dry the petals.

5. Select eleven petals that look good together— these will be used for this project. Apply copper foil and burnish.

6

7

8

9

Construct the Pendant

6. Cluster five petals around the bottom of the largest of the centerpieces.

7. With the flux brush, place a drop of flux between each petal, near the centerpiece.

8. Taking care not to move the pieces, tack-solder the petals together near the centerpiece. This is best accomplished by dripping hot solder between the petals (rather than touching the iron to the copper foil) while holding the petals in place with a pointed object such as a pencil. Let it cool before continuing.

9. Solder the front of the pendant. Let it cool.

10. Solder the back of the pendant. Let it cool.

11. With a light touch, solder the rim of the pendant.

(Continued on next page)

11

ECO-TIP **Conserving Water**

Before we apply copper foil to stained glass components, glass pieces must be washed with dishwashing liquid to remove all traces of cutting oil. When we cut glass with a tile nipper, no oil is used, and washing with dishwashing liquid is not required. Instead, keep a bowl of water next to the grinder and toss in each petal after grinding. After you've finished grinding, retrieve the petals and dry them. The water is still clean and can be saved for your next project, added to your grinder to top off the water level, or used to water your plants.

Prepare a Wire Loop

12. Cut a 3.5" (9 cm) piece from the silver wire. With your fingers, bend it to an angle slightly wider than the bottom of the centerpiece.

13. With the pliers, gently curve each side of the wire so that it lies along the edge of the centerpiece. Bend the ends so that they cup the bottom of the centerpiece. With the wire cutter, remove the extra where the wires overlap under the centerpiece.

14. Remove the wire from the pendant back. Hold the wire to the workboard with the pliers. Wipe flux on the bottom half of the wire and apply a thin layer of solder.

Add the Wire to the Pendant

15. Place the pendant facedown on the center of the workboard. Hold the wire in place with the pliers against the back of the pendant.

16. Tack-solder one side of the wire to the pendant back. Turn the pendant face up and verify that the wire is in the correct position. Adjust if necessary by widening or closing the angle of the untacked side of the wire.

17. Turn the pendant facedown. Tack-solder the free end of the wire to the back of the pendant. Let cool.

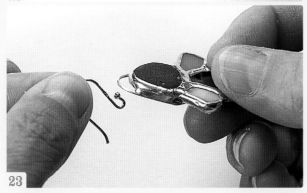

18. Solder all the wire to the back of the centerpiece, taking care to let the solder on one side cool before soldering the other side.

19. Wash the pendant with dishwashing liquid and water, and dry. With the brass brush, burnish any solder that appears to have white spots.

20. Apply finishing compound. String the chain through the top wire.

Construct the Earrings

21. Using one of the smaller centerpieces and three petals, construct the earring, following Steps 6–11.

22. Cut a 2½" (6.5 cm) piece from silver wire. With the pliers, bend the piece to an angle slightly wider than the bottom of the centerpiece.

23. Repeat Steps 13–19 with the earring and the wire. Apply finishing compound. Slide the earring onto an earring hook.

24. Repeat Steps 21–23 to construct the second earring.

Stained Glass Hibiscus
STUDIO PROJECT ## Treasure Box

Combine your fusing and stained glass skills to make a tropical treasure box. It's the perfect box for special photographs or keepsakes and a unique, personal gift that will be cherished.

MATERIALS

Fusing Glass

- 1 oval of opaque purple, 3" × 4" (7.5 × 10 cm)
- 2 rectangles of opaque pink, 1" × 1½" each (2.5 × 4 cm)
- 1 rectangle of opaque pink, 1" × 2" each (2.5 × 5 cm)
- Dichroic fusing scraps

*COE Alert: All the fusing glass for this project must be from the same COE family.

Stained Glass

- 1 sheet of green glass, 12" × 12" (30.5 × 30.5 cm)
- ½ sheets of red, pink, and purple glass, 12" × 6" (30.5 × 15 cm) each
- Glass nuggets, jewels, prisms, other embellishments *(optional)*
- Kiln shelf paper
- Pattern paper
- Prepared hinge, 5²⁄₃" (14.5 cm) long
- Copper foil
- Flux
- Solder
- Patina *(optional)*
- Finishing compound
- 2 pieces of silver wire, 18 or 20 gauge, each 2" (5 cm) long
- Nylon-wrapped jewelry wire, about 16" (40.5 cm) long
- 4 crimp beads

TOOLS

- Burnisher
- Cotton balls
- Cutting pad
- Flux brush
- Fusing kiln
- Glass cutter
- Glass grinder
- Latex gloves (if using patina)
- Pattern shears
- Pencil/waterproof marker
- Pliers
- Soldering iron
- Tile nipper

SKILLS REVIEW

- Creating and Using Patterns, *page 50*
- Constructing Boxes, *page 69*
- Making Hinges, *page 59*
- Finishing Techniques, *page 56*
- Firing Schedules, *see note, page 80*

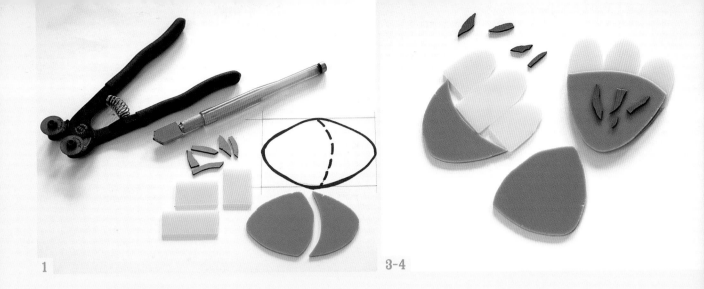

1

3-4

INSTRUCTIONS

Prepare the Fused Flower Center

1. With a glass cutter, cut an arch from corner to corner across the oval of purple fusing glass.

2. With a tile nipper, round one end of each of the three rectangles of pink fusing glass. Grind to a smooth edge.

3. Lay the smaller purple piece on shelf paper in your kiln. Nest the pink pieces in the curve. If the pink pieces are too wide for the base, trim them slightly and regrind.

4. Cover all four pieces with the larger purple piece, aligning the corners. Place decorative scraps of fusing glass on top of the purple glass. This will become the flower center. Full-fuse to create the flower center, using the firing schedule appropriate for your glass.

5. After firing, wash the flower center of any residue and grind any sharp edges. Dry well.

Prepare the Stained Glass Box Base

6. From the green stained glass, cut four rectangles, each 2" × 6" (5 × 15 cm), and a 6" (15 cm) square. Construct the box. Wash and dry the box; don't apply finishing compound. Set aside.

Prepare the Stained Glass Lid

7. With the pencil, draw a 7" (18 cm) square on pattern paper. Place the fused flower center about two-thirds of the way up on the right side, with the pink petals pointing toward the upper right-hand corner, extending slightly outward from the pattern square. Trace the fused flower center to mark its location in the pattern.

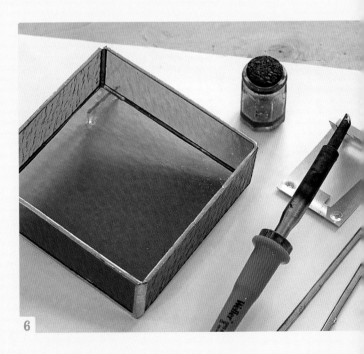

6

8. Using the pattern shown here as a guide, draw the pattern as follows: From the bottom of the fused flower center, draw a sweeping curve downward and left to the edge. From three points on each side of the fused flower centerpiece pattern (top, middle, and bottom), draw arches toward the edges, rounding them to form petals around the flower center. Add embellishments if desired. Keep a straight edge on the left side and bottom of the lid pattern. Verify that all pattern shapes can be cut from glass; alter the pattern if needed.

9. Use the waterproof marker to trace the final lines of the lid pattern. Mark up the pattern to indicate glass colors: The upper petals should be red, the middle petals pink, and the lower petals purple. Remaining pieces should be green. If you'll be using glass with a pattern, mark the design flow on the petal patterns.

10. Cut the pattern pieces with the pattern shears.

11. With the glass cutter, cut the glass according to the pattern pieces. Grind, wash, and foil all pieces. Solder the lid together.

12. Solder the outer tubing of the prepared hinge to the left side of the lid, evenly centered.

13. Quickly run the soldering iron down the outside of the hinge to clean off any extra solder.

14. Wash and dry the lid; don't apply finishing compound.

(Continued on next page)

Finishing

15. With the pliers or your fingers, twist pieces of silver wire into right-angle loops.

16. Solder one loop into the upper right-hand corner of the box where the base meets the sides.

17. Position the second loop on the underside of the lid about 2" (5 cm) from the right edge and at least 1" (2.5 cm) below the top edge, over a seam. Carefully solder the loop into place.

18. Slide the unsoldered hinge arms into the hinge tubing on the lid. Retrieve the base and set the lid on it. Verify that the arms rest on the side seams when the lid sits well. Adjust if needed.

19. Without removing the arms from the hinge tubing, tack-solder one arm to the box's side seam; verify that the lid still sits as desired before soldering the second arm. Return to the first arm and complete soldering. Be very careful not to solder any part of the hinge arms to the lid, or any part of the lid to the side of the box.

ECO·TIP | Wiping vs. Washing

As you work on a project, you'll want or need to wash your work between steps. You can save water by wiping the glass with a damp cloth or paper towel instead of washing it in the sink. If you need soap to remove oil or flux, use a premoistened towelette, such as those sold to clean babies' hands. After you've cleaned the piece, dip the cloth in water, squeeze it out, and go over your piece again to remove any soap residue. When cleaning after applying patina, always do a full wash with dishwashing liquid, toothbrush, and water.

23-25

25

(detail)

20. Wash the box with dishwashing liquid and water, and dry it well, handling the lid with care.

21. If you'd like to stain the metal seams of your box with black or copper patina, put on latex gloves and apply patina to the seams with a cotton ball. Wait twenty minutes for the patina to soak into the metal, and then repeat Step 20.

22. Slide two crimp beads about 2" (5 cm) onto one end of the jewelry wire. Slip the end of the wire through the silver loop in the base and fold back. Slide the crimp beads back down the wire, capturing the end of the wire. Crimp shut, firmly. Slide two crimp beads onto the other end of the wire.

23. Open the lid to a 90-degree angle and hold it gently in place with one hand. Avoid opening the lid at a wider angle so as not to stress the hinges.

24. With your free hand, slip the unattached end of the wire through the silver loop on the underside of the lid. Fold the extra wire over and verify that the wire will hold the lid about 1" (2.5 cm) more than 90 degrees. (If the wire is too short, the lid will drop closed unless you hold it open manually. If the wire is too long, the weight of the lid can wrench and tear the hinge.)

25. Slide the open crimp beads up to capture the end of the wire and crimp firmly shut. Cut off any extra wire.

26. Wipe all the seams with finishing compound on a cotton ball.

Recycled Bottle
STUDIO PROJECT
Necklace

Combine your torch skills with your love for the environment and string your necklace with lampwork beads forged in the flame from recycled bottle glass.

MATERIALS

- 3 empty bottles (wine or beer) of different colors
- Bead separator
- Leather lace or fiber cord, 22" (56 cm) long
- Purchased jewelry findings:
  – 1 lobster clasp
  – 1 jump ring
  – 2 large crimp bands with built-in end ring

TOOLS

- 2 pairs of heavy pliers
- 2 pairs of jewelry pliers
- 30 mandrels
- Bead reamer
- Clean cloth or beading sponge (for sorting beads)
- Glass cutter
- Hemostat *(optional)*
- Lampworking kiln
- Lampworking safety glasses
- Lampworking torch

- Metal ruler
- Old towel
- Regular safety glasses
- Waterproof marker

SKILLS REVIEW

- "Programming a Digital Controller," *page 28*
- "Cutting Glass," *page 43*
- "About Mandrels," *page 95*
- "Making a Basic Bead," *page 102*
- "Disks and Hollow Beads," *page 107*
- "Heat Mapping," *page 99*
- "Cleaning Beads," *page 99*

INTRODUCTION

Working with a New Material: Recycled Bottle Glass

Discarded glass bottles are everywhere, and it's far better to recycle or reuse them than to throw them in the garbage. Wine, beer, and water bottles come in a wide range of greens, browns, and blues and can be used to make attractive, eco-friendly beads.

Working with bottle glass isn't simple—you must first prepare the glass for use. The pieces will be curved, irregularly shaped, and hard to hold. Bottle glass melts slowly and often spits and cracks in the flame, no matter how carefully you heat it. As a safety precaution, wear a long-sleeved shirt and make sure that anyone observing you while lampworking wears safety glasses and long sleeves and sits somewhat behind you. The exact COE of bottle glass is never guaranteed, and bottle beads should be annealed with a unique schedule. See note, page 127.

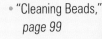

From left to right: jewelry findings, pliers, a hemostat, mandrels, industrial safety glasses (for use when cutting bottles), leather lace, and three wine bottles in different colors.

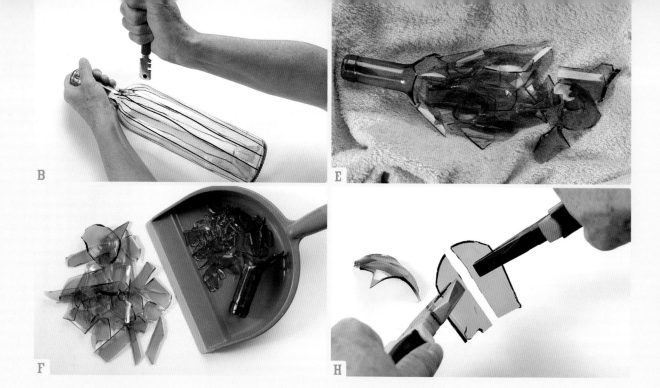

INSTRUCTIONS

Prepare the Bottle Glass

The harvesting process is time-consuming, so much so that I rarely prepare the glass on the same day as I use it to make beads. For this reason, this specific process has been labeled separately from the rest of the project as Steps A through J.

A. Select one bottle. Peel off the label and wash away any adhesive. Use the waterproof marker to draw stripes down the sides of the bottle from the neck to the base. Each stripe should be no wider than 1" (2.5 cm).

B. While sitting, grasp the bottle neck firmly in your lap with your nondominant hand and score down each stripe with the glass cutter, dipping the glass cutter in cutting oil between scores. Don't worry if you don't cut exactly along the lines, as long as each score runs from the neck to the base.

C. Wrap the scored bottle in the towel so that the entire bottle is enveloped, to prevent glass shards from shooting out later. Bring the bottle outside. Put on safety glasses and sit on a hard surface, such as a patio or sidewalk.

D. Holding the wrapped bottle by the neck, swing it up and bring it down with moderate force onto the sidewalk or patio. You should hear glass break.

E. Unfold the towel and examine the results. If the bottle is largely intact, rewrap the bottle and repeat Steps C and D with lighter force.

F. Pick through the pieces. Discard the bottle neck and all pieces smaller than your thumb. There will be large pieces that didn't break along the score lines.

G. To break a piece that didn't break along its score line, use the metal jaws of the heavy pliers to tap on the inside of the piece, under the score.

H. Grasp both sides of the piece with the heavy pliers as close to the score line as possible. Snap along the score away from you. Repeat as necessary.

I. Wash the pieces with dishwashing liquid and water to remove cutting oil and any organic residue. Dry. Any marker lines left will burn off in the torch.

J. Repeat Steps A–I for each bottle. After washing and drying, store each color separately.

Bottles come in a surprising array of colors. Store each color separately after breaking.

Make the Beads

1. Prepare thirty mandrels with bead separator and set them to dry for at least one hour.

2. Program the kiln with the annealing schedule provided for bottle glass.

3. Light the torch and put on safety glasses.

| TIP | **Programming the Lampworking Kiln**

A special annealing schedule should be used when kiln-annealing bottle glass. View and download the author's annealing schedule for bottle glass from her website **www.glassandlight.blogspot.com**. You can also go to Quarry's website at **www.quarrybooks.com**, search for *The Glass Artist's Studio Handbook,* and find a link to it there.

1

(Continued on next page)

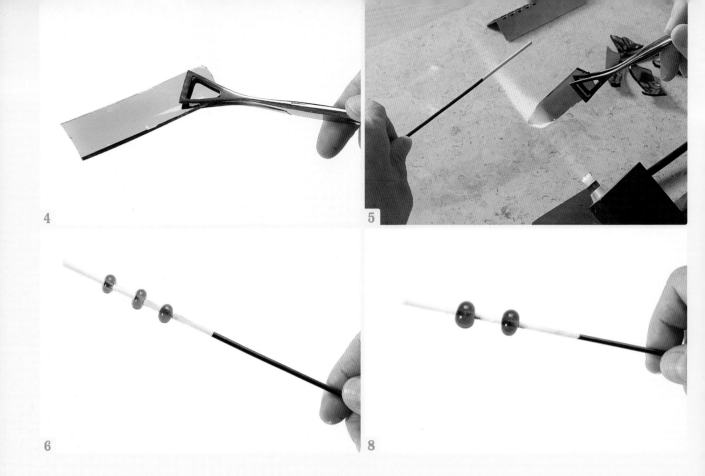

4. Select several strips of bottle glass from the bottle of the lightest color. Grasp one piece with the hemostat or heavy pliers.

5. Introduce the piece slowly into the flame, at the tip where it's cooler, before bringing it closer to mid-flame. If it spits or cracks as you bring it toward the torch, return it to the tip of the flame and heat it some more.

6. Moving to the center of the flame, make twelve simple spacers with two wraps of glass each. To conserve mandrels, it's possible to make two or three spacers on each mandrel if you work quickly.

7. Keep spinning the beads on the mandrel until the glow has died. Place them in the hot lampworking kiln.

8. With the same colored glass, make six larger spacers, each with three wraps. It's possible to make two spacers on each mandrel if you work quickly.

9. Select several strips of bottle glass from the bottle of the darkest color. Grasp one piece with either the hemostat or pliers.

10. Build two disks on the mandrel, ½" (1.5 cm) apart. If you're not sure of the distance, check against the ruler before starting the second disk.

11. Build the edges of the disks toward each other until they touch.

12. Seal the space between the disks, melt well, and make a hollow bead.

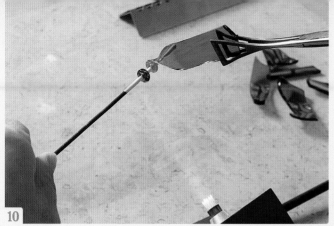

10

11

12

14

17

13. Continue spinning. Move the hollow bead to the end of the flame.

14. Heat more glass and decorate the hollow bead with dots and ribbons. Heat at the end of the flame just enough to bond the decorations to the bead.

15. Keep spinning the bead on the mandrel until the glow has died. Place in the hot lampworking kiln.

16. With the same color (dark) glass, repeat Steps 10–13 to create two hollow beads; don't decorate them. Place them in the kiln.

17. Using glass from the remaining (midtone) bottle, make six large spacers with five wraps of glass each, following Steps 5–7.

18. Shut down the torch. Follow the kiln's instructions to manually Skip the firing program to Step 2 and start the annealing process.

19. After annealing has finished and the kiln has returned to room temperature, remove the beads from the kiln, and separate them from the mandrels. Clean the beads and the mandrels, and let them air-dry.

(Continued on next page)

Construct the Necklace: Add the Clasp

20. Fold 1" (2.5 cm) of the end of the lace. Slide a crimp band onto the folded end of the lace, with the end ring extending beyond the lace. With pliers, press firmly to flatten the band securely onto the lace. Trim the extra lace if desired.

21. Using the jewelry pliers, open the jump ring.

22. Slide the lobster clasp onto the jump ring. Slip the jump ring through the end ring of the crimp band.

23. With the pliers, close the jump ring.

Construct the Necklace: String the Beads

24. Lay the clean beads in a line, on a clean cloth or beading sponge. The darkest, largest bead (the decorated hollow bead) should be in the center. One dark hollow bead, undecorated, should be on either side.

25. Place three midtone beads on either side.

26. Place nine light-toned beads on either side, with the smallest beads at the ends.

27. Examine the line of beads and make any adjustments you desire, including removing beads or changing their location.

28. Starting at one end of the line, with the smallest bead, string all the beads onto the lace.

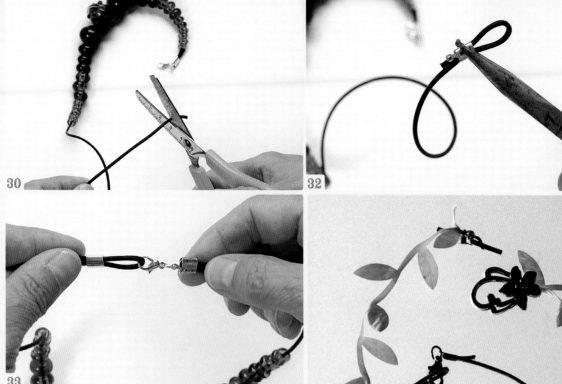

30

32

33

Construct the Necklace: Create the Clasp Loop

29. Grasping the lace firmly, hold the necklace around your neck to check the length of the lace. Alternatively, measure it against another necklace with an attractive length.

30. Trim the lace to the desired length, allowing an extra 1" (2.5 cm) to form a loop at the end.

31. Slide the crimp band onto the end of the lace, with the end ring facing toward the lace.

32. Fold 1" (2.5 cm) of the end of the lace. Slide the crimp band over the loose end. With the jewelry pliers, press firmly to flatten the band securely onto the lace.

33. To close the necklace, catch the leather loop in the lobster clasp.

Mix and match recycled glass to make different necklaces. On the left is a necklace made from two wine bottles, a broken vase, and leather lace. On the right is a necklace made from a beer bottle and a scrap of salvaged cloth trim.

Beaded Stained Glass Panel:
STUDIO PROJECT Jurassic Jewel

Ammonites were sea creatures that lived during the Jurassic era, along with their better-known cousin, T-Rex. Today, ammonite fossils can be purchased halved and polished—a fascinating reminder of Earth's ancient history. Fossils are often protected, so be sure to buy them only from reputable dealers who sell legally harvested ammonites.

MATERIALS

For the Beads

- 2 rods of 96 COE lampworking glass in sand, white, or beige
- Raku frit
- Bead release

For the Stained Glass

- 1 sheet of blue green glass, 9" × 4" (23 × 10 cm)
- 1 sheet of brown glass, 10" × 10" (25.5 × 25.5 cm)
- Copper foil
- Flux
- Solder
- Finishing compound
- Cotton balls
- Pattern paper
- Copper patina

OTHER MATERIALS

- 1 roll of 18-gauge silver-plated wire
- 2 pieces of medium-weight brass wire, each 6" (15 cm)
- 4 pieces of medium-weight brass or steel wire, each 10" (25.5 cm)
- 1 chain, 10" to 12" (25.5 to 30.5 cm) long
- 20 purchased seed beads from glass or metal
- Uncoated jewelry wire
- 1 ammonite, halved

TOOLS

- 7 mandrels
- Burnisher
- Cotton balls
- Craft knife
- Cutting pad
- Disposable gloves
- Flux brush
- Frit tray
- Glass cutter
- Glass grinder
- Lampworking glasses
- Lampworking kiln, vermiculite, or fiber blanket
- Lampworking torch
- Marver
- Metal snips
- Needle-nose pliers
- Pattern shears
- Pencil, paper, ruler, eraser
- Permanent marker
- Regular pliers
- Rod rest
- Safety glasses
- Scissors
- Soldering iron
- Soldering rag

SKILLS REVIEW

- "Common Stained Glass Processes," *page 50*
- "Creating and Using Patterns," *page 50*
- "Working with Wire," *page 57*
- "Lampworking," *page 92*
- "Basic Bead Shapes," *page 102*

This project combines stained glass, bead weaving, and lampworking materials and techniques. If you don't practice lampworking, replace the bead materials with five purchased tube beads.

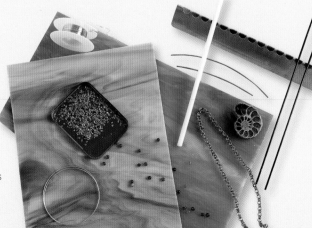

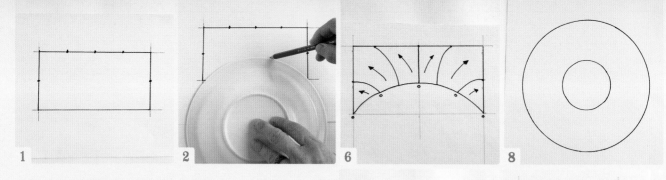

1 2 6 8

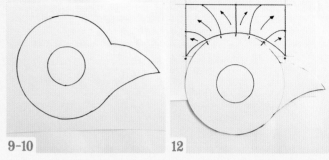

9-10 12

Design Tip for Making Your Work Stronger

The halved ammonite fossil decorating the hanging bridge of this project also strengthens it. If you prefer not to use a real ammonite in your design, replace it with a large glass nugget, a small agate slab, or a disk of glass.

INSTRUCTIONS

Create Pattern 1: The Hanging Bridge

1. On a piece of pattern paper, use the pencil to draw a 3" × 6" (7.5 × 15 cm) rectangle. Mark dots along the top at 1½" (3.75 cm) increments. Mark a dot on each side, about halfway up.

2. Draw an arch from the bottom-left corner to the bottom-right corner. (If you find it difficult to draw the arch, use the edge of a plate as a stencil.)

3. Add a centerline from top to bottom, using the finished pattern shown in Step 6 as a guide.

4. Add two graceful arches from the bottom to the top on each side of the centerline to divide the pattern into four pieces.

5. Add two graceful arches from the bottom to the side to divide the pattern into six pieces.

6. Trace the pattern with the permanent marker. If your blue green glass has a visible design flow, mark the pattern pieces to indicate which way the flow should run. Photocopy or trace the pattern to create a second pattern to use as a reference. On the reference pattern, draw five circles representing the five metal loops—one on each lower corner, one in the center, and one on each side, in the seam closer to the corner.

Create Pattern 2: The Stained Glass Ammonite

7. On a piece of pattern paper, draw a circle that is 5" to 6" (12.5 to 15 cm) in diameter. (Small soup bowls, canisters, and large jar lids can be used as a stencil.)

8. In the center of the circle, add a second circle about 2" (5 cm) in diameter.

9. Following the bottom curve of the outer circle, extend the pattern about 2" (5 cm), and then continue the line back toward the circle's perimeter.

10. Trace the perimeter of the pattern in permanent marker.

11. Cut out the pattern with scissors.

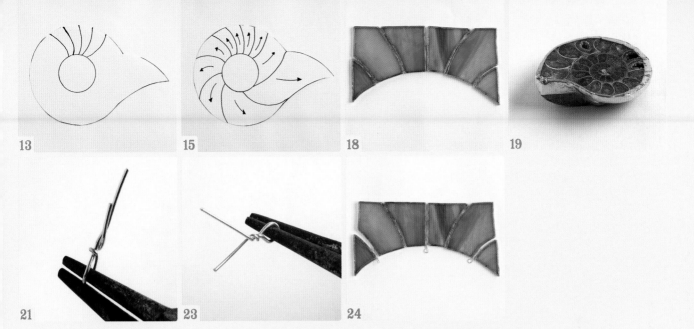

13   15   18   19

21   23   24

12. Position the ammonite pattern piece inside the arch of the hanging bridge and note where the cutting lines meet the edge. Mark these on the ammonite pattern in pencil.

13. From the center of the ammonite, draw arches that meet the marks.

14. Add several more arches around the ammonite.

15. When you're satisfied with the overall look of the ammonite, trace the arches in permanent ink. Number the pieces, if you wish. If your brown glass has a visible design flow, mark the pattern pieces to indicate which way the flow should run. Photocopy or trace the pattern to create a second pattern to use as a reference.

Prepare the Hanging Bridge

16. With the scissors, cut out the perimeter of the hanging bridge pattern. With the pattern shears, cut out the pattern pieces.

17. Cut the pattern pieces from the blue green glass, paying attention to the direction of the design flow, if relevant.

18. Grind all the pieces. Wash with dishwashing liquid, and dry well. Wrap with copper foil. Burnish and position according to the bridge pattern.

19. Wash and dry the ammonite fossil (or other, see tip box). Wrap with copper foil and burnish. Set aside.

20. With the metal snips, cut a 2" (5 cm) piece of silver-plated wire.

21. Hold the wire with the needle-nosed pliers and bend in half. Twist the wires together, forming a small loop around the pliers. The stem of the loop should be twisted all the way down.

22. Repeat twice for a total of three wire loops with a twisted stem.

23. Repeat twice more, but twist the wires only at the top, leaving the wires to form an angle that will fit around the corner pieces.

24. Slide the three closed stem wires between the pieces of glass, leaving only the loops exposed.

25. Adjust the pattern pieces to accommodate the wire, verifying that the top line of the bridge is straight.

26. Set the two open stems aside.

(Continued on next page)

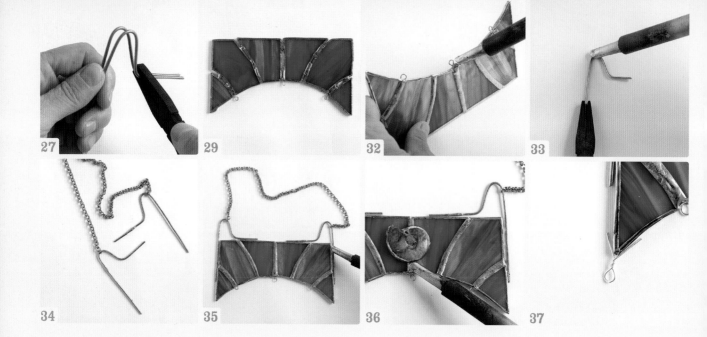

27. Hold the two pieces of 6" (15 cm) brass wire together. With regular pliers, bend the wires to a 25-degree angle, about halfway down the wire. Slide the pliers farther down the short end of the wire, and bend back. Adjust so that the angle is 90 degrees. The wires should lay flat. Set aside.

28. Turn on the soldering iron and wet the soldering rag.

29. Tack-solder the hanging bridge, capturing the silver wires between the pieces.

30. Full-solder the bridge front.

31. Full-solder the bridge back.

32. Solder the rim, taking care not to get solder in the wire loops.

33. Retrieve the bent brass wires. On the worktable, superheat a wire with the hot soldering iron. Apply flux and a thin layer of solder to all the wire. If the solder does not stick well, heat the wire some more. Turn over, and apply solder to the other side. Repeat to coat the second wire with solder.

34. String the chain onto the coated wires.

35. Position the wires on the top corners of the bridge. Solder into place.

36. Brush flux onto the ammonite and apply a thin coat of solder to all the copper foil on both sides. Solder the ammonite (or alternative) flat side down onto the centerline of the bridge, affixing it top and bottom to the seam.

37. Retrieve the open stemmed loops; position them around the corners. Solder into place.

38. Wash and dry the bridge. Avoid wetting the chain.

39. Set the bridge aside.

Construct the Stained Glass Ammonite

40. Cut out the pattern pieces for the ammonite with the pattern shears.

41. Trace the pattern pieces onto the brown glass, taking advantage of the glass's visual design flow.

42. With the glass cutter, cut out the pattern pieces.

43. Grind all the pieces. Wash them with dishwashing liquid and water and dry well.

44. Apply copper foil and burnish.

45. Position each piece according to the pattern.

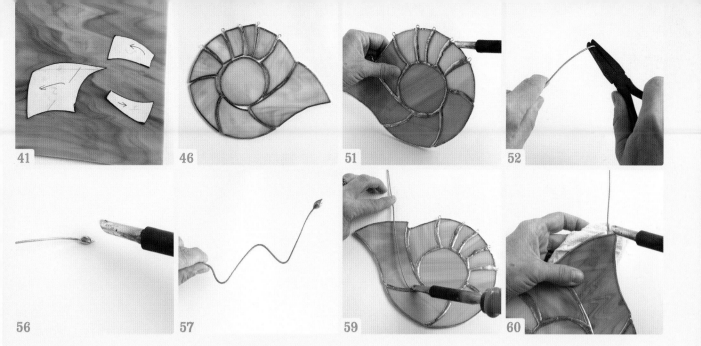

46. Follow Steps 20 and 21 to make five wire loops. Insert them between the pieces on the top of the ammonite pattern. Adjust the pieces as needed.

47. Turn on the soldering iron and wet the soldering rag.

48. Tack-solder the ammonite, capturing the silver wires between the pieces.

49. Full-solder the ammonite front.

50. Full-solder the ammonite back.

51. Solder the rim, taking care not to get solder in the wire loops.

Prepare the Ammonite Arms

52. With the pliers, make a small bend in the end of one piece of 10" (25.5 cm) medium-weight wire.

53. Position the wire against the back of the ammonite so that the small bend rests on a seam. The wire should lay flat against the glass. With the marker, mark the wire where it crosses the ammonite's edge.

54. With the hot tip of the soldering iron, superheat the last inch (cm) of the wire, including the small

bend you made in Step 52. Brush on flux and apply a layer of solder to the area that you superheated.

55. Superheat the wire around the ink mark. Add flux and apply a layer of solder to both sides of the wire.

56. Superheat the straight end of the wire. Apply flux and a thin layer of solder. When cool, add a large drop of solder. Let it cool around the end of the wire.

57. Using your fingers, bend the wire to create squiggles.

58. Repeat Steps 52–57 to create a total of four ammonite arms.

59. Position the four arms on the back of the ammonite so that each bend at the end of the arm rests on the seam. Solder each arm into place.

60. Turn the ammonite face side up. Rest the ammonite against the damp soldering rag at the edge where the wires protrude. Add a drop of solder to the edge where each wire crosses it to hold the wires in place.

61. Wash the construction with dishwashing liquid and water. Dry well.

(Continued on next page)

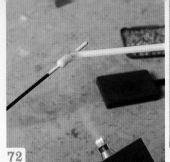

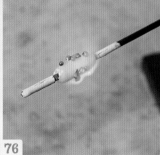

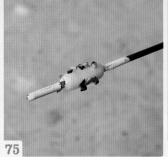

Apply Patina

62. Wearing disposable gloves, apply copper patina with a cotton ball to the ammonite and the hanging bridge, wiping acid onto all the seams and soldered areas. Avoid getting patina on the chain.

63. Let the ammonite rest twenty to forty minutes.

64. With a toothbrush, dishwashing liquid, and water, scrub pieces; avoid wetting the chain. Dry well.

65. With the cotton balls, apply finishing compound to all the metal of both constructions.

Make the Lampwork Beads

66. Dip seven mandrels in bead separator. Set to dry.

67. Program the lampworking kiln with the annealing schedule for 96 COE glass, and turn it on.

68. Prepare the torch station with the glass rods, the marver, and a frit tray. Pour some raku frit into the tray. Keep an open canister of water within reach.

69. Put on lampworking safety glasses. Light the torch.

70. Grasp a glass rod in your dominant hand and a mandrel in your other hand.

71. Introduce the glass to the flame slowly by poking it in and out of the tip of the flame. Spin the mandrel in the flame to heat it. When the glass begins to glow, bring it toward the center of the flame.

72. Touch the hot end of the glass rod to the mandrel. Spin the mandrel, gathering glass. Continue heating glass and adding it to the mandrel until you've made a tube bead.

73. Melt the tube bead until it's smooth. If you have trouble making an even tube, roll it against the top of the marver to shape the hot glass.

74. While the bead is still glowing, roll it in the frit.

75. With many frits, including raku, it's better to have too little frit than too much, so try to collect just a little on the bead. If the frit doesn't stick to the surface of the bead, the bead is too cold; reheat the bead and try again.

76. Bring the bead into the center of the flame, and melt the frit into the bead until it's very smooth. Once the bead is hot enough, you should be able to see the surface of the raku changing, although its colors won't be obvious.

77. Remove the bead from the flame and hold it over the water in the canister to cool it quickly. Don't touch the water with the mandrel or the bead.

78. The raku colors should appear. If they're mostly brown, return the bead to the end of the flame and heat just a little. Cool again. Repeat until greens and purples begin to show.

79. When you're satisfied with the raku colors, flash the bead at the end of the flame to even up the heat throughout the glass.

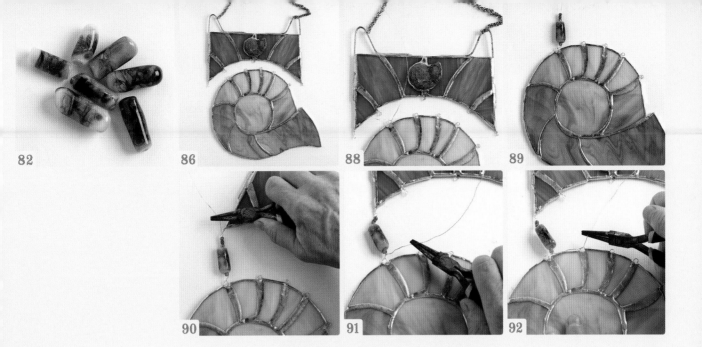

82

86

88

89

90

91

92

80. Remove from the flame, still spinning, and let cool until the bead has lost its glow.

81. Place in a hot lampworking kiln, between layers of fiber blanket, or into vermiculite.

82. Repeat Steps 70–81 until you've created seven beads.

83. Manually Skip the kiln firing program to the next step and begin the annealing process.

84. After the firing is finished and the kiln has returned to room temperature, remove the beads from the mandrels. Clean them under water to remove all traces of bead release.

85. Select five beads to weave into the panel.

Weave the Beads between the Panels

86. Working on a clean table, position the bridge and the ammonite as they should hang.

87. Cut 4 to 5 feet (1.5 m) of jewelry wire.

88. Slip 3" (7 cm) of jewelry through the ammonite's left loop. Twist the jewelry wire closed several times. Leave the short tail of wire turned up.

89. String one seed bead, one raku bead, and three more seed beads onto the free end of the wire. Slide them down to the end so that they slide over the short tail, hiding it, and are resting near the ammonite.

90. Slip the wire through the left loop of the bridge. Pull it all the way through so that the gap between the ammonite and the bridge is filled with beads. String the wire through the silver loop again. Grasp the wire with the needle-nosed pliers and pull tight to hold the wire in place. As you pull the wire, untangle any loops before they form a knot or kink in the metal wire.

91. String the wire back down through the same three seed beads, one raku bead, and one seed bead. Pull the wire taut. String the wire through the silver loop again and pull tight to hold the wire in place.

92. Moving to the next silver loop on the ammonite, slip the jewelry wire through the loop and pull it taut. Slip it through the loop again, pulling taut to hold the wire in place.

93. Repeat Steps 89–92 until all five beads have been strung. Finish at the ammonite's right loop with several twists of wire. String the extra wire up through the beads a third time. Cut off the excess where it exits the top bead for an invisible end.

Stained Glass Kaleidoscope:

STUDIO PROJECT # Fantastic Journey

Create a conversation piece—your very own kaleidoscope from mirrors and art glass. You can fill the end chamber with transparent glass scraps, beads, and other small items such as transparent stones and tiny cut glass jewels.

MATERIALS

- 3 pieces of mirror, each 1" × 5" (2.5 × 12.5 cm)
- 3 pieces of opaque art glass, any color, each 1½" × 5¼" (4 × 13.5 cm)
- 3 pieces of opaque art glass, any color, each 1¾" × ¾" (4.5 × 2 cm)
- 2 squares of clear window glass, 2" × 2" (5 × 5 cm)
- 1 piece of opaque art glass, 2" × 2" (5 × 5 cm)
- 1 piece of "milky" glass, 2½" × 2½" (6.5 × 6.5 cm)
- Small scraps of transparent art glass, transparent beads, cut glass jewels, crystals, etc. (for the end chamber)
- Wires, nuggets, beads, glass scraps (for decorating the outside of the kaleidoscope) (optional)

- Electrical tape
- Copper foil
- Flux
- Solder
- Patina (optional)
- Finishing compound
- Cotton balls

TOOLS

- Burnisher
- Cotton balls
- Cutting pad
- Flux brush
- Glass cutter
- Grinder
- Paper towels or pre-moistened towelettes (optional)
- Permanent marker
- Pliers (optional)
- Scissors
- Soldering iron
- Thin rod such as a wooden skewer, mandrel, or knitting needle
- Tile nipper

SKILLS REVIEW

- "Common Stained Glass Processes," *page 51*
- "Constructing Boxes," *page 69*

TIP **Introducing New Materials**

In this project, we add milky glass and mirrors to our portfolio of materials. Art glass mirrors, like regular mirrors, are backed with a reflective material. Silver refers to the common backing. It's not recommended to use colored mirror for the kaleidoscope because it will darken the reflections. Always cut mirror from the glass side, and take great care when grinding the edges so as not to chip the backing. The backing must be thoroughly dry before applying copper foil, or stains will appear in the backing along the mirror's edge. Milky glass is window glass that has been acid-etched or sandblasted on one side. It lets in all the light while obscuring what is beyond it. For this reason, it's often used to close the ends of kaleidoscopes. Milky glass is best cut on the untreated side.

Kaleidoscopes require many pieces because they're constructed with an inner mirrored tube, a decorative outer casing, and an end chamber filled with baubles.

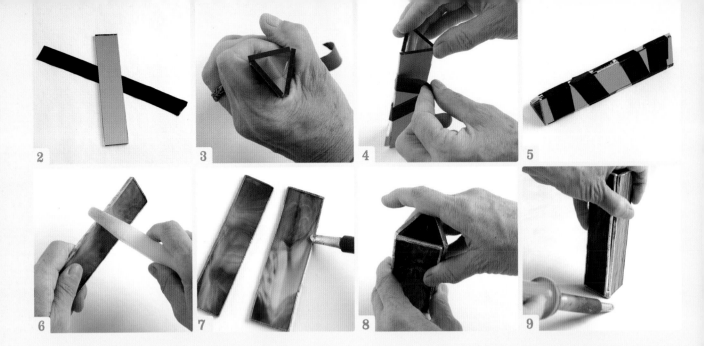

INSTRUCTIONS

Prepare the Mirrored Tube

1. Wash the mirrors to remove all ink, oil residue, and dirt. Dry them thoroughly. Don't grind unless the edges are very uneven. Don't apply copper foil. Polish the glass side of the mirrors with a clean cloth or paper towel until there are no streaks visible. Lay the mirror pieces glass side up.

2. Cut a piece of electrical tape about 4" (10 cm) long. Lay it sticky side up on the table. Place one piece of mirror on the tape, mirror side up (backing against the tape) and at an angle. With clean, dry hands, press the mirror onto the tape.

3. Grasp the three pieces of mirror in your hand so that they form a three-sided tube standing upright on the table. Adjust so that the bottom of the tube is even and the corners meet. The reflective side of the mirror should be on the inside of the tube; the backing should be on the outside of the tube.

4. Wrap the ends of the electrical tape around the tube, adhering firmly.

5. Cut two more pieces of electrical tape. Adjusting the mirrors so that the sides meet, tape the mirrors in two more places.

Construct the Outer Casing

6. Grind the three long pieces of art glass. Wash with dishwashing liquid and dry. Apply copper foil and burnish.

7. Bush flux onto all the seams and rims. Apply a thin layer of solder to all the foil. Wash the three pieces with dishwashing liquid and dry very well.

8. Grasp the three pieces of opaque glass in your hand so that they form a three-sided tube, standing upright on the table. Adjust so that the bottom of the tube is even and the edges form strong corners. Verify that each piece of glass is set so that the side you want displayed is on the outside of the tube.

9. Tack-solder one corner at the bottom, without flux.

10. Rotate the tube and tack-solder each corner after gently adjusting the placement, if necessary, to form a strong corner, until all three corners have been tack-soldered. Don't use flux.

11. Turn the opaque tube over and repeat Steps 9–10.

12

15

17

18

19

12. Without using flux, full-solder the top seam of the opaque glass tube. Add just a little solder at a time and let it cool between applications to avoid overheating the seam and dripping solder into the casing. When finished, the seam should be completely covered and the solder should be full and nicely rounded.

13. If, after soldering, the soldered seam isn't smooth, sparingly wipe flux onto the seam and heat the seam slightly. This should be done only after the seam is fully soldered to prevent flux from getting inside the chamber, where it's hard to clean.

14. Rotate the tube to position an unsoldered seam on top. Solder the seam without flux. Repeat for the last seam.

15. If solder has dripped into the casing, let it cool and remove it. In many cases, it will separate from the glass when it cools and can be easily shaken out of the casing. If there are jagged bits of solder stuck to the inside seams, pointing into the inside of the casing, melt them flat.

16. With a damp paper towel or premoistened towelette, wipe down the seams to remove any dirt, and dry.

17. Hold a square of window glass over the end of the tube. Using the marker, draw a triangle the same dimensions as the end of the chamber.

18. With the glass cutter, cut the clear glass cap from the window glass. Trim the corners with the tile nippers, if you wish. Grind, wash, dry, and foil it. Brush on flux and add a light layer of solder to all the copper. Wash with dishwashing liquid and dry well.

19. Solder the rim of the window glass to the outer seams of the end of the tube to form a clear glass cap. Don't use flux.

20. With a damp paper towel, wipe down the seams to remove any dirt, and dry.

(Continued on next page)

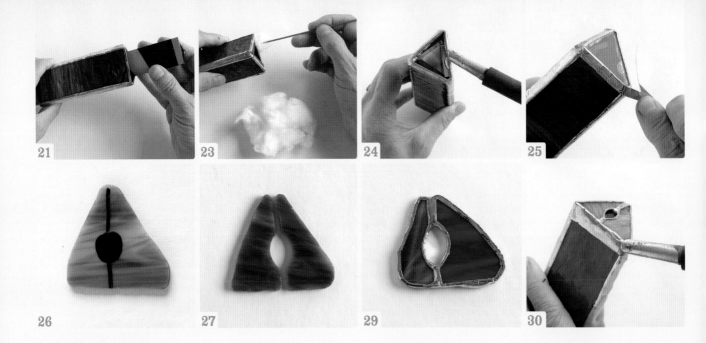

Construct the Mirrored Chamber

21. Without removing the tape from the mirrors, slide them into the open end of the casing until they reach the end. Don't bang the glass cap.

22. If the mirrors don't slide easily into the casing, rotate them and try again. It's also possible to turn the casing around and put the opposite end into the casing first.

23. To prevent the mirrors from moving or sliding in the casing, shred some cotton balls. With the thin rod, push bits of cotton between the mirrors and casing until the mirrors are held firm.

24. Following Steps 17–20, cap the open end of the casing with clear glass.

25. If the edge is uneven, add a strip of copper foil to cover the gap. Use flux very sparingly, and solder the corners before soldering the rest of the exposed copper foil. The solder must cover the copper foil and melt smoothly into the existing seams but not enter the casing at any point.

Construct the Eyepiece

26. From the 2" × 2" (5 × 5 cm) square of opaque art glass, cut a triangle the same dimensions as the first cap. With the marker, draw a dividing line down the center. Add a circle.

27. With the glass cutter, cut the triangle down the middle, along the marker line. With the tile nipper, clip out a very small part of circle from both pieces. Grind both pieces, spending extra time grinding the small center circle to create a viewing hole in the center of the eyepiece.

28. Wash the eyepiece parts with dishwashing liquid, dry well, and wrap with copper foil.

29. Solder the eyepiece parts together, taking care not to fill the hole in the center with solder. Wash with dishwashing liquid and dry well.

30. Polish the clear cap on one end of the kaleidoscope's chamber. Place the eyepiece over the clear cap. Solder the eyepiece to the edges of the clear cap without using flux.

32

33

34

35

Construct the End Chamber

31. Grind, wash, and dry the three remaining pieces of opaque art glass. Apply copper foil.

32. Stand the three pieces in the shape of a shallow triangle, making strong corners. Tack-solder into place.

33. Solder the inside and the outside of the triangle as well as all the rims.

34. Cut a piece of milky glass the same dimensions as the triangle. Cap the triangle with the milky glass, following Steps 17–20. Wash the construction and dry well.

35. Turn the end chamber construction over so that it makes a little dish. Fill it one-half to three-quarters full with clean, small bits of transparent glass, crystals, beads, and items such as tiny plastic flowers.

36. Position the mirrored chamber over the open end chamber with the eyepiece on top. Without using flux, tack-solder the two parts together on all sides.

37. Without using flux, full-solder the casing to the end chamber. Take care not to drip flux into the chamber. Clean the seams and glass with a damp cloth, paper towel, or premoistened towelette, and dry.

37

40

Finishing

38. If you wish, use glass, beads, and wires to embellish one or two of the sides (the kaleidoscope will rest on the third side). Solder with a very light hand so as not to melt the existing seams.

39. If patina is desired, apply with a cotton ball to all the solder except the eyepiece. Wait twenty minutes before washing off the acid. *Do not wash the entire piece with dishwashing liquid and water. Wipe with a damp, soapy cotton ball or premoistened towelette so as not to dirty or wet the glass cap under the eyepiece.* Dry well.

40. Apply finishing compound to all the seams, taking care not to get oil or wax on the glass cap or under the eyepiece.

To use the kaleidoscope, look through the eyepiece while facing a strong light. Turn the kaleidoscope to change the pattern.

Floral Lampwork Necklace:
Spring Beauty

Craft glass flowers and leaves in the torch to create a unique and lovely necklace. This project combines glass, imagination, and pearls in a strong, feminine design.

MATERIALS

- Glass
- 1 sheet of marbled green fusing glass, 8" × 12" (20.5 × 30.5 cm), for leaves
- 1 sheet of transparent fusing glass, any color, 1¼" × 8" (3 × 20.5 cm), for petals
- 1 opaque lampworking rod, any color, for the flower base
- 1 opaque lampworking rod, in a contrasting color to the flower base (optional)

OTHER MATERIALS

- 1 string of freshwater pearls
- Nylon-wrapped jewelry wire, 24" (60 cm)
- Crimp beads
- Bead release
- 1 silver toggle clasp

* COE Alert: All the glass (fusing and lampworking) must be from the same COE, since they will be combined in the beads.

TOOLS

- 10–20 mandrels
- BBQ lighter
- Bead reamer/pipe cleaners
- Blue Runner
- Clean cloth (for sorting beads)
- Cutting pad
- Glass cutter in jar with cutting oil
- Jewelry pliers
- Lampworking kiln, vermiculite, or fiber blanket
- Lampworking safety glasses
- Lampworking torch
- Marver
- Masher
- Permanent marker
- Rod rest
- Ruler
- Scalpel
- Tile nipper
- Tweezers

SKILLS REVIEW

- "Cutting Glass," page 43
- "Lampworking," page 92
- "Annealing Schedules," see note, page 92

The leaves and flowers for this necklace are made from fusing glass. The design combines glass beads with pearls and silver.

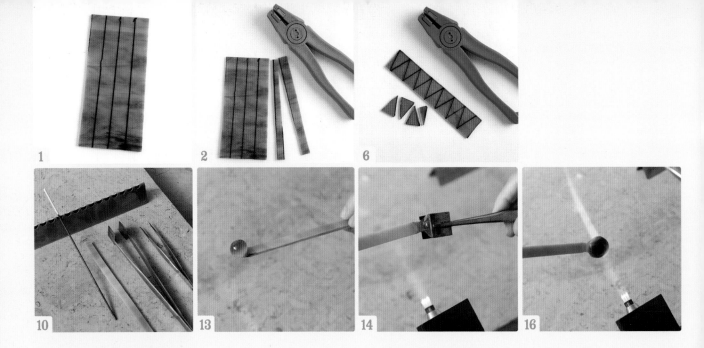

1 2 6

10 13 14 16

INSTRUCTIONS

Prepare the Glass

1. Place the green fusing glass on the cutting pad. With the marker, draw strips ½" (about 1 cm) apart.

2. With the glass cutter and Blue Runner, cut the glass along the stripes.

3. Carefully wash the strips with dishwashing liquid and water. Rinse well and dry.

4. Shake out the cutting pad over the garbage and return it to the workboard.

5. Place the transparent fusing glass on the cutting pad. With the marker, divide it into triangles that are ¾" (2 cm) wide and 1¼" (3 cm) tall.

6. Score the glass with the glass cutter, and break apart with the Blue Runner. You'll need at least five petals for each flower bead.

7. Handling them carefully, swish the triangles in soapy water. Rinse in clean water and dry. You don't need to wash off the ink—it will burn off in the flame.

Make the Leaves

8. Dip all the mandrels in bead separator. Set to dry.

9. Program the lampworking kiln with the annealing schedule appropriate for your glass, and turn it on.

10. Prepare the torch station with the strips of green glass, the masher, tweezers, and one prepared mandrel. An open canister of water should be within reach.

11. Put on lampworking safety glasses and light the torch.

12. Grasp a strip of green glass in your dominant hand. Introduce it to the flame slowly by poking it in and out of the tip of the flame. When the glass begins to glow with heat, bring it toward the center of the flame.

13. Heat the end of the strip until it becomes soft. Tilt the strip so that the glass melts back onto itself. Keep melting and turning the strip until you have a ball of hot glass at the end, at least the size of a marble. The leaves don't have to be identical, so the size of the glass ball doesn't have to be precise.

14. Catch the ball of hot glass between the blades of the masher, and squeeze the ball flat.

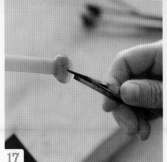

17.

19.

21.

22.

26.

29.

15. Release the glass and dip the masher in the canister of water to cool it before returning it to the table.

16. Heat the bottom half of the mashed glass until it's glowing with heat.

17. With the tweezers, grasp the hot glass and slowly pull it into a leaf shape, twisting a bit as you pull.

18. Let the glass cool for a moment, and then reposition the tweezers to grasp the leaf firmly.

19. Move the glass so that the flame flows across the glass strip about 1" (2.5 cm) before the leaf starts. Usually the sudden heat will shock the glass and it will break. If it doesn't break spontaneously, melt through the strip to remove the leaf.

20. Heat the head of the leaf and the leftover tab of glass until they're glowing and soft. Pick up the mandrel from the rod rest and heat it in the flame.

21. Holding the leaf so that it's perpendicular to the mandrel, touch the hot glass to the mandrel. Wrap the hot glass around the mandrel to make a bead.

22. When the hot glass is wrapped on the mandrel up to the head of the leaf, rotate the leaf so that the bead is behind the leaf. Let it cool until the glass stiffens and the leaf doesn't move.

23. Place the leaf in the kiln, in the vermiculite, or between the fiber blankets.

24. Repeat Steps 12–23, moving a prepared mandrel to the rod rest each time, until all the mandrels have been used to make leaves.

25. Manually Skip the digital controller's firing program to Step 2 and begin the annealing process.

26. After the firing is finished and the kiln has returned to room temperature, remove the beads from the mandrels. Clean them under water to remove all traces of bead release. Let dry.

Make the Flower Bead

27. Dip a mandrel in bead separator and set it to dry.

28. Program the lampworking kiln with the annealing schedule appropriate for your glass, and turn it on.

29. Set up the torch station with tweezers, the marver, the scalpel, the lampworking rods, and the prepared mandrel. Set the glass triangles on the marver. An open canister of water should be within reach.

30. Put on lampworking safety glasses and light the torch.

31. Grasp the opaque glass rod in your dominant hand. Introduce it to the flame slowly by poking it in and out of the tip of the flame. When the glass begins to glow with heat, bring it toward the center of the flame.

(Continued on next page)

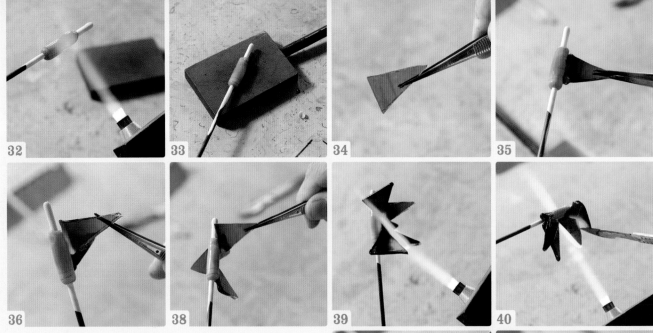

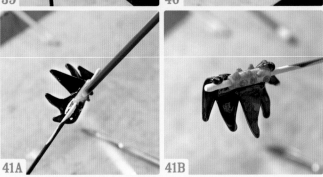

32. Heat the end of the rod until it becomes soft. Make a tube bead that is at least 1" (2.5 cm) long.

33. If you have trouble making the shape, roll the hot glass on the marver.

34. With the tweezers, pick up a triangle of glass, holding the pointy end of the triangle.

35. Introduce the glass to the flame by flashing it in the flame. When the shorter edge of the triangle starts to glow, position it standing on the tube bead, along the center line. Apply heat where the triangle meets the bead. When the join begins to melt together, release the tweezers.

36. Pick up a second triangle. Repeat Step 35, but position the triangle layered just over the first triangle. The left corner of the second petal should be in the center, and the triangle should be angled slightly. If the triangle droops too much, lift it with the scalpel.

37. Repeat Steps 34–36, positioning the third triangle on the left, layered just over the first triangle.

38. Repeat Steps 34–36, attaching two more triangles, with a gap between triangles four and five.

39. Bathe each triangle in the flame, softening the edges and melting them a bit. (Work on one triangle at a time.)

40. Use the tweezers and the scalpel to gently lift and turn the hot glass, sculpting the triangles into flower petals as you wish.

41. If desired, add contrasting dots to the base bead where it's visible at the top of the flower.

42. Flash the flower in the end of the flame several times.

43. Place the bead in the kiln, in the vermiculite, or between the fiber blankets.

44. Manually Skip the firing program to the next step and begin the annealing process.

42   46   48   49

50   51   52   53

45. When the firing is done and the kiln has returned to room temperature, remove the mandrel from the bead. Clean the flower in water with a bead reamer to remove any bead release. Let dry.

String the Necklace

46. Lay all the materials and tools for stringing the necklace on a clean table: flower bead, leaf beads, pearls, nylon-wrapped jewelry wire, jewelry pliers, crimp beads, toggle clasp, and scissors.

47. Measure the jewelry wire against a favorite necklace to determine the length you desire. Cut the wire to the desired length with scissors.

48. Separate the two parts of the toggle clasp.

49. Slide two crimp beads onto one end of the wire. Slip the wire through one half of the toggle. Fold the wire back, capturing it with the crimp beads.

50. With the jewelry pliers, firmly press the crimp beads until they're flattened and the wire is immovable. Set the wire aside.

51. On a soft, clean cloth, position the glass beads as they should appear when strung. The flower

54

bead should be in the center. An equal number of leaves should be placed on each side of the flower bead, with the larger leaves in the center.

52. Place two to four pearls on each side of the flower. Distribute more pearls between the leaves as you like.

53. Starting at one end of the line of beads, string all the beads and pearls onto the jewelry wire in the order that they're positioned on the cloth.

54. Slide two crimp beads onto the end of the wire. Slip the wire through the other half of the toggle. Fold the wire back, capturing it with the crimp beads.

55. With the jewelry pliers, firmly press the crimp beads until they're flattened and the wire is immovable.

Glass Artist
Gallery

Janet Hill
ARTIST PROFILE

Janet Hill's first studio was a length of kitchen counter, a table, and a bookshelf. As her skills and experience grew, so did her studio. Eight years after the first time she held a glass cutter, she has taken over her son's old bedroom and turned it into a small and compact studio.

Tools and supplies are stored nearby and "everything has a home." Janet believes that one benefit of a small space is that there are no wasted steps. She uses one main work surface interchangeably with a waffle grid for cutting glass and an old cork bulletin board for soldering. She keeps her ring saw and grinder in a tool chest and tucks her mosaic cabinet (once a kitchen cupboard) under her worktable. A lot of her studio furniture can be folded up and put away when not in use. Last but not least, her son's little closet is now a built-in storage unit that houses glass, books and patterns, and all manner of found objects that will be incorporated into future projects.

Janet surrounds herself with things that inspire her, such as colorful pieces of art, cheerful pictures, and good music. "I love the entire creative process, from the first spark of an idea, to unveiling the finished piece of art, and everything in between. For me, the whole process is exhilarating and therapeutic!"

"Find a space you can dedicate entirely to your craft, even if it's small, and make it your own. Everything after that is pure joy!"

Katsushi Fukuta
ARTIST PROFILE

Katsushi Fukuta started his professional life as an engineer. He taught himself the basics of stained glass and studied sumi-e—traditional Japanese ink painting. He enriched his techniques with a journey to France, where he learned the arts of fusing and painting on glass, eventually creating a style of his own that has proven both beautiful and popular.

Katsushi's message for new artists is not to isolate themselves from the community at large. "To make good art, we must have a good nature. To have a good nature, we must connect with many people who have experienced life and have strong values."

ARTIST PROFILE # Aimee Mitchell

Aimee Mitchell describes her creations as stained glass mosaics. Her projects range from large wall art to tiny jewelry. Her home studio is one room only—and she chose the room with the largest window and the most natural light.

Her studio has abundant and creative storage solutions: old spice racks for jewelry findings, coat hangers for hanging finished art, and dish dryers for storing glass. Aimee has positioned an old bookcase at the side of her table to hold her grouts, glues, and such. "When working with mosaics," she says, "you always seem to be acquiring things to use in your art, so storage is key."

"Surround yourself with the things you love."

ARTIST PROFILE
Mette Enøe

A professional artist whose "artmosiac" techniques have been recognized in Denmark and internationally, Mette Enøe taps into her imagination and combines glass, metal, and stone to create unique glass art. She started small, at her family's dinner table; today Mette works in a sunny studio with an outdoor pavilion to attract visitors and display her creations. Her designs and techniques are not only unique, they're copyrighted.

Her most important tools are her glass cutter and a large worktable. Her worktable is mounted on wheels and raised to reduce back strain. Her kiln is large, with separate controls for the lid and sides, giving her more process options. Because Mette's home studio lacks ample space, the kiln is in the basement. "On cold days," she explains, "it helps heat the house." Her least successful glass studio purchase was a glass saw; it was messy and loud, and after two years, she gave it away.

Her recommendation for setting up a new studio is to focus on space—something she was in short supply of for a long time. "You must have a room with some space around you. You will always find that you will need more space than you expected, particularly for storage and displays. You can display your artwork in another room, but you'll want to have your materials close to you."

"In our house, we ask our children and all our guests to keep their shoes on, because small bits of glass could be anywhere. We don't want any accidents!"

Kristy Sly

ARTIST PROFILE

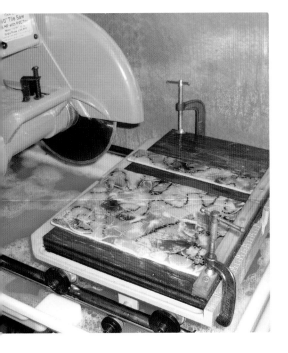

Kristy Sly is an independent artist who creatively combines fusing, cold cutting, hot work, and silk screening with enamels to create her glass art.

"My studio is a wonderful place. I have a large fabrication table [4' × 8' (1.2 × 2.4 m)] where I draw, design, cut glass, and do much of my work. Under the table is a large shelf for storing my trade show booth materials, scrap glass, and works in progress. Along one wall, I have magnificent floor-to-ceiling shelves of differing heights and lengths... Each material has its own made-to-fit location... I try to have a place for everything and everything in its place to maximize space in my small in-home studio."

Kristy's studio has expanded to include her basement, which houses her kilns and tile saw, and her garage, where she stores her back stock. Every room has crates and shelves full of glass and fusing supplies.

Kristy's tip for new fusing artists is to buy or build the biggest kiln you can afford, because "you can always make a small piece in a big kiln, but the inverse is not true." She also recommends focusing on getting lots of natural light into the studio.

ARTIST PROFILE

Laura Tarbutton

Laura Tarbutton got her start as a crafter when she was very young. "Growing up in the countryside of rural Mississippi, I always had busy hands and nature to guide me; beautiful oak trees, majestic pines, and lots of animals were my inspiration." Her studio, The Beach House, is a teaching studio, with a fun and creative atmosphere that welcomes students. To save money, she and her husband built it themselves from an old farmhouse that was already on their property, and painted the walls with cheap, leftover paint that they bought on sale.

Laura stores her glass and tools in old metal cabinets and an antique closet purchased at a local auction. The front room of The Beach House is her gallery and largest classroom. Her personal studio has stations for slab pottery, lampworking, PMC, and enameling. Laura has a small kiln for firing metal clay and enamels, and annealing lampwork beads. The kitchen is a perfect setting for the larger tools she needs to craft with metal and clay. Laura teaches bead weaving, jewelry making, and metal clay work as well as dichroic cab fusion and cold connections.

Her most important tip for beginners: "Don't be afraid to ask. Some artists are protective of their techniques, but for every artist who is closed-mouthed, two others are proud to share tips, ideas, and encouragement."

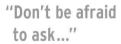

"Don't be afraid to ask..."

ARTIST PROFILE

Susan Cooley

ARTIST PROFILE

Susan Cooley left a career in environmental work to become a full-time stained glass artist. Her studio encompasses a lot of the great outdoors. Susan deliberately chooses organic materials to complement her glass; flowers, assorted grasses, tree branches, driftwood, moss, rocks, and crystals are her favorites.

"Many of my ideas come to me while out hiking, paddling my kayak, and skiing in the backcountry. My camera comes with me everywhere as I use photographs to inspire my designs."

To manage her business, Susan keeps a well-organized office, filing projects in progress, displaying general and detailed calendars, and maintaining a library of glass art books. Her whiteboard lists supplies to order and daily tasks.

One of Susan's many excellent ideas: "Get in the habit of cleaning up your studio after each use and put your tools away. This keeps your studio from getting very messy. You'll save money in the long run because you'll always know where your tools are." It will also make your studio a safer place to work!

Teresa
ARTIST PROFILE Laliberte

Teresa Laliberte is a full-time lampwork artist, specializing in highly decorative and detailed sculptural beads. Her first studio was in a cellar. Eventually, Teresa upgraded to a charming garden shed that she and her husband put together in their backyard from a kit.

Because the shed is constructed from wood, fire proofing was very important. "We bought a length of heat-resistant countertop which we covered with ceramic floor tiles." They furnished Teresa's studio with inexpensive shelving and PVC tubing to hold her glass rods. She stores her photography equipment there, too.

Teresa says, "I outgrew this studio in about three months—we should have bought a much larger shed." Large enough, she adds, to put in some insulation. "Since the walls are only thin wood, these little houses get incredibly hot in the summer and freeze in the winter." And while the bare-wood finish has lots of rustic charm, Teresa recommends finishing yours with paint or varnish, because the bare wood has worn out fast.

Her tip for those new to glass: "Don't lose hope of learning if classes aren't a possibility for you. I can tell you firsthand that learning on one's own is certainly possible, because that's how I did it. It just means that you'll have to work a bit harder."

April Burgess

April Burgess doesn't have a formal studio; instead, she works in her dining room, where the view of Pikes Peak fills her with inspiration. "I really enjoy the comfort of working out of my home. It gives me the freedom to set my own pace and create the perfect working environment." She stores her supplies and inventory in her garage, where she works on her larger pieces.

Although she had been crafting all her life, she pushed her dream of being a "real artist" to the back of her mind and dedicated her life to her family and a career. In 2008, April lost her job. Rather than mourn her loss, she was inspired to let her creativity blossom. Her first mosaics were for the home and for friends. Eventually she started selling and now markets her work online.

April believes that each piece she creates is destined for someone special who so happens to be looking for exactly the thing she has created.

Her first tip for those new to glass: "Surround yourself with positive people." She also urges us to let our creativity flow: "God gave each of us special talents for a reason; they are meant to be shared."

> "God gave each of us special talents for a reason; they are meant to be shared."

Isabella Raven

ARTIST PROFILE

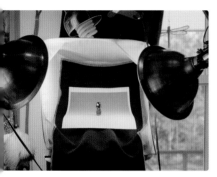

Isabella Raven's journey as a crafter and artist started in childhood, and her first sales were made while she was still in high school. After living in many places and working with many materials, she moved to her current home in the Florida Mountains of Massachusetts. She and her son fireproofed the garage floor, put in some windows, and added a ventilation system, and she happily settled into making glass beads in a structure she called a "Barley Box," a fireproof frame around her lampworking area that includes exhaust vents, storage opportunities, and items that bring her inspiration.

The garage studio had a lot of drawbacks: The winters were bitterly cold, sometimes cracking her beads even while they were in the kiln, and making it difficult to work. Last year Isabella moved her studio into her home. "It is so nice to be able to create my lampwork beads all year round!" The move gave her a chance to better organize her glass, her storage, and her studio lighting.

Rather than using didymium lampworking safety glasses, she wears a special face shield so that she can wear her regular prescription glasses while she works. "It took a few days to adjust to it, but it's been a great investment." Isabella works with an oxygen concentrator rather than O_2 tanks.

One of Isabella's special features worth noting is her photo cube, a dedicated photography station with mobile lighting fixtures and the right materials and background to absorb glare. She takes all her own photographs, but credits her husband for giving her a good digital camera and teaching her how to use it.

ARTIST PROFILE
The Elbaz Family

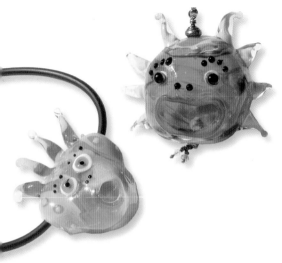

Robyn Keller Elbaz and her husband, Amnon Elbaz, started making stained glass art in 1980; at that time, stained glass supplies couldn't be purchased in Israel, so they manufactured their own lead came and forged colored art glass in a handmade furnace. In the mid-1990s, Amnon changed direction and began making glass beads and designing flameworking tools. Robyn and their three children, now grown, were the first of his many lampworking students; today, each member of the Elbaz family creates beads with a personal and distinct style, and Amnon continues to develop new, high-quality tools which are offered on the global market. Robyn and their daughter, Shani, create unique lampwork jewelry and interior décor accessories.

Robyn notes that, "like most lampwork artists," their studio is very small. To maximize wall storage, the torches are set up in the center of the room; a swivel chair puts everything easily within reach. But while their space may be limited, they've set up for safety in a very big way.

Amnon has constructed a complex ventilation system. The venting hood spans the length of the entire table—two full torch stations—and efficiently sucks away potentially harmful fumes and expels them outside. The vent is paired with a small window fan to bring in fresh replacement air. They've also done a great job of fireproofing their studio. All gas cylinders are stored outside (as required by law), so they have emergency shut-off valves installed within reach of the torches. A vial of lavender oil provides quick relief for burns.

Their tips for lampworking artists: "Don't think that opening a window or outside door is sufficient. Not so!" Amnon also cautions against placing the center of the ventilation hood directly over the flameworker, which could blow fumes back into the artist's face. As a last safety tip, Robyn and Amnon point out that carpeting shouldn't be used in a lampworking station. Stone, concrete, or ceramic tile is fireproof and easy to clean.

"Headaches are a sign that your ventilation system is not working as it should."

Natalie Hahn

ARTIST PROFILE

Natalie Hahn is a self-taught glass artist; her "love affair" with glass struck at the age of twelve. Over the years, she has practiced stained glass, fusing, and other cold and warm glass techniques in garden sheds, porches, dining rooms, and an open carport. Eventually, she recycled materials from a local dump to enclose the carport, creating a much-needed and weatherproof work area, and to construct a retail studio in her yard, the Glass Shack.

Natalie's studio is on the small side, but she has organized it to accommodate four kilns, a welding station, a lampworking torch, an airbrushing station, and an area where she creates and stores large architectural stained glass panels as well as her other works in progress.

Much of her furniture does double-duty; her three worktables are all built with shelving for storage, and her glass grinder shares space with a handcrafted light box.

Natalie's tip: "Always remember that most techniques have been around for many years. Anything is possible, and I hope my studio, work, and environment showcase what can be done on a modest budget."

> "Glass is a magical medium, and one of the most gratifying arts."

ARTIST PROFILE
Maxine Chivers

Maxine Chivers has taken a keen interest in art since childhood. After taking a "short break" to have two children, work, and run a house, she discovered a book on lampworking. Her style has developed with the help of local and master's classes and many hours of practice, all fed by her quirky sense of humor and fondness for cartoons.

Her studio is set up in a corner of her garage: "While I would dearly love a studio loaded to the hilt, here I sit among my husband's collection of hot-rod parts, our cars, and my vintage motorbike. It is not the most spacious setup…"

Maxine stores her glass rods in a collection of vintage jars, some of which belonged to her husband's grandmother. "My glass sits well within reach if I have a whim to use any particular color while I am creating. Plus, if I draw a creative blank, I can often find inspiration looking at the glass jars as the light catches them through the window."

Her first tip for people new to glass is about tools, and is simple: Try before you buy. "I can't tell you how many tools or presses I have bought, only to discover I don't like using them."

Kerri
ARTIST PROFILE Fuhr

Kerri Fuhr's creative spirit is fueled by her love of animals: She has raised or cared for a fascinating variety, including lionhead rabbits, yaks, lynxes, miniature horses, and exotic chickens. Her childhood was spent on the top of a mountain in British Columbia, a lush location that her family shared with bears, eagles, and other woodland animals. Today, she pours her passion for nature and wildlife into her glass beads. Kerri uses glass stringers—fine threads of colored glass—the way other artists use paints, creating intricate designs and decorations from melted glass.

Now, Kerri shares her work space with three steadfast studio mascots: Baily, Benny, and Lucy. Her studio is more than just a workplace: "It's my own little haven from the world where I can dream and create in a magical space all my own." Inspired by Moroccan art, Kerri painted the studio walls in warm terracotta colors, laid a tile floor, and brought in Moroccan lanterns for light. Her decorating style is exotic, boasting textiles from India and Uzbekistan and Buddha statues from Indonesia. She made her first bead in late 2000; since then, Kerri has developed a unique lampworking style which has won her much acclaim and several prestigious awards. Making glass beads is her full-time job. Her advice to new glass crafters is to surround yourself with things that inspire you. "My studio is full of paintings and sculptures of ravens and crows since they are one of my favorite subjects to depict on my beads!"

ARTIST PROFILE Lori Bermann

Loris Bermann must be the envy of many crafters and artists, because she has two studios—one in her house for scrapbooking and paper crafts, and one in her garage for lampworking. Her lampworking studio is compact, but includes everything she needs. She added a metal, fire-proof top to an engineer's drafting table, and tucked filing cabinets and shelves underneath for storage.

When she left graphic design for melting glass, she brought with her a black tool caddy with a swivel base, where she stores her tools and special glass rods. Galvanized containers meant for flower arrangements hold mandrels. When Lori remodeled her kitchen, she snagged the old cabinets and installed one over her table, where it holds most of her glass rods.

If Lori has a motto for new crafters, it might be, "Small is beautiful!" Her studio proves that you don't need a lot of space to have a lot of creativity.

"Small is beautiful!"

Emma Mackintosh

ARTIST PROFILE

Emma Mackintosh describes her home studio as "packaway" —everything can be easily stowed when not in use. Located in the beautiful English Lake District, Emma's torch station is next to a large window, which is great for lots of natural light and inspiration. "Being next to the window, and its wide windowsill, also means that I can store all my frit (and I use a lot of frit!) on the sill and have all my tools within reach." Her studio is small and she welcomes her family and friends who often drop in to see her work. "I think my studio does show that it is possible to work with glass even if you don't have unlimited resources or space."

Emma takes recycling seriously and her storage and work station solutions often incorporate her care for the environment; glass rods are stored in used jam jars, frit in discarded herb containers. Her work table was built by a friend from scraps of old wood.

Emma advises, "Don't rush into buying lots of expensive equipment; many tools can be improvised. While there are a lot of tempting presses, mashers, and gadgets available, it's best to first spend time with glass, learning how it flows with heat and what it can do."

Lisa-Jane

ARTIST PROFILE Harvey

Lisa-Jane Harvey has a small teaching studio in Auckland. Working with soft glass, she instructs her students in the arts of fusing, lampwork, cold working, and glass casting. A main concern for her studio is ventilation—every lampworking station needs two hoods to collect the impurities released by melting glass (one at ceiling height and another below the table) that vent to the outside. "Naturally," Lisa-Jane points out, "the ceiling hoods must be well secured so that they won't drop onto the table!" In her experience, a kitchen hood for the ceiling and a "laundry style" extraction fan should be adequate for most home studios.

Lisa-Jane's tip for new lampworking studios: "There must be enough space behind your chair to ensure that you can quickly stand up and step back should any hot glass land on your lap." She also shared a tip with us for proper disposing of the water you have soaked your beads in before removing them from your mandrels, noting that it should never be poured down the drain. "Pour it in your garden or on your neighbor's lawn or flower bed, instead."

Deirdre Briley

ARTIST PROFILE

Deirdre Briley is a glass artist with a sense of whimsy and great imagination. Her studio is located in her home's two-car garage. "It's the best and safest place," she says, "to work with molten glass and smelly fumes."

Deirdre started with a simple torch and fiber blankets to cool her beads. She gradually upgraded from fiber blankets to a used annealing kiln. She recently added a second kiln, "new, this time." Her hand tool list includes salvaged items such as dental picks, eyebrow tweezers, and pedicure scissors. She admits to being a garage sale goddess and addicted to thrift stores, searching for tools and studio furniture like the newspaper boxes she stores her glass in. Her proudest purchase is her vent ("to suck out all those nasty fumes"), which is actually an oven hood. A portrait of Einstein reminds her that "Imagination is more important than knowledge" and a disco ball is ready when she feels the need to dance.

"Life is so much better
with a smile on your face!"

Resources

Type Lampworking, Fusing, Mosaics, or Stained Glass into your favorite search engine and you'll undoubtedly receive hundreds of links. This list includes my favorites, but there are many others for you to discover.

General All-Supply Stores

www.delphiglass.com—art glass and supplies
www.yglass.com—stained glass supplies
www.spectrumglass.com—stained glass and fusing
www.bullseyeglass.com—fusing and lampworking
www.alpineglass.com—stained glass and fusing
www.howacoglass.com—lampworking
www.waleapparatus.com—lampworking and glass blowing
www.sundanceglass.com—hot glass work

Specialty Suppliers

GLASS

www.valcoxfrit.com—specialty frit for lampworking
www.dichro-wonderglass.com—dichroic glass
http://myworld.ebay.com/mxkhk—crystals in many shapes, sizes, and colors; click on "Items for sale" or "View Store"
http://myworld.ebay.com/condan—cut glass jewels and glass cabs for stained glass work; click on "Items for sale"
http://stores.ebay.com/Mosai-Yak-Mosaic-Tile—glass nuggets (three sizes) and pressed glass cabs
www.thompsonenamel.com—enamels for lampworking; select by COE

EQUIPMENT AND TOOLS

www.hotheadsource.com—**Hot Head** torch manufacturers and specialists
www.zooziis.com—cool lampworking tools such as bead presses, curved mandrels, and door knob kits
http://romazone.etsy.com—hard-to-find lampworking tools including hemostats

OTHER SUPPLIES

Robinann41@hotmail.com—D-Lead soap and unleaded solder
Info@greenisrael.co.il—custom multiuse "eco" bags
Rainboroc@aol.com—raw and polished gemstones and unusual items such as sharks' teeth; also see eBay listings at **http://myworld.ebay.com/rainboroc** (click on "Items for Sale" or "View Store")
http://stores.ebay.com/tribalgh—handmade beads direct from Africa
http://stores.ebay.com/Northern-Stones—sliced agates and stone beads
http://beadboxman.etsy.com—display boxes for lampwork beads
http://stores.ebay.com/balli-silver-jewelry—wholesale silver jewelry findings
www.discountbeadstore.com—metal beads and jewelry findings

Helpful Information and Organizations

www.cdc.gov/niosh—National Institute of Occupational Safety and Health (NIOSH); search for "glass" or "glass studio" to access reports)
www.warmglass.com—fusing
http://stainedglass.org—stained glass
www.isgb.org—lampworking
http://etsyglass.com—artists' collective
www.self-representing-artist.com—glass artists group
www.americanmosaics.org—mosaics

Educational Centers

http://penland.org—Penland School of Crafts
www.publicglass.org—Public Glass
www.nationalglasscentre.com—National Glass Centre
www.glassfurnace.org—The Glass Furnace
www.pilchuck.com—Pilchuck Glass School
www.oatkaglass.com—OATKA School of Glass and Glass Studio
www.contempglass.org/links/linkschools.html—Art Alliance for Contemporary Glass (a general list)

Contributing Artists

Lori Bermann
Maple Valley, WA 98038
www.loribergmann.blogspot.com
page 10, 16, 40, 168 (Artist profile)

Deirdre Briley
14500 Fagerud Road SE
Olalla, WA 98359
maxkat@wavecable.com
www.AnkleBiterBeads.etsy.com
page 171 (Artist profile)

April Burgess
Mosaic Art & Unique Creations
aburgess37@comcast.net
www.ABurgessShoppe62407.etsy.com
page 162 (Artist profile)

Maxine Chivers
Glass By Girlfriday
Central Coast NSW Australia
girl _ friday1962@yahoo.com.au
www.girlfriday1962.etsy.com
Facebook: GlassByGirlfriday
page 15, 166 (Artist profile)

Susan Cooley
Akasha Fine Art Glass
8-622 Front St.
Nelson, BC, Canada V1L 4B7
susan@akashaglass.ca
skcooley@shaw.ca
www.akashaglass.ca
www.akasha-fine-art-glass.blogspot.com
www.linkedin.com/in/SusanCooley
page 160 (Artist profile)

Robyn & Amnon Elbaz
LBaz Creations
Givat Zeev, Israel
elbaz@bezeqint.net
www.lbazcreations.com
page 17, 31, 164 (Artist profile)

Mette Enøe
Haslev, Denmark
www.glaspatch.dk
www.glasmatch.dk
page 22, 157 (Artist profile)

Kerri Fuhr
Aldergrove, BC, Canada
www.kerrifuhr.com
page 167 (Artist profile)

Katsushi Fukuta
5-2-6 Nakanedai
Ryugasaki-shi, Ibaraki
301-0002 Japan
k.fukuta@tappu.com
www.tappu.com
www.tappu.etsy.com
page 155 (Artist profile)

Natalie Hahn
RedTail Glass Works
PO Box 773
Freeland,WA 98249
redtail@whidbey.com
www.redtailglassworks.com
page 14, 152, 165 (Artist profile)

Lisa-Jane Harvey
Born to Bead
12 Minaret Drive
Bucklands Beach
Auckland, New Zealand
www.borntobead.co.nz
page 170 (Artist profile)

Janet Hill
2419 Cooper Ave.
Colorado Springs, CO 80907
newmoonglass@q.com
www.newmoonglass.etsy.com
page 154 (Artist profile)

Hot Head Source
www.hotheadsource.com
page 30, 96

Teresa Laliberte
LavendarCreek Glass
Germany
teresa@lavendercreek.de
www.lavendercreek.de
page 161 (Artist profile)

Emma Mackintosh
1 Elder Ghyll
Hawkshead, Cumbria, UK
beads@theflyingbead.co.uk
www.theflyingbead.co.uk
page 169 (Artist profile)

Menachem "Mano" Matos
Kibbutz Tirat Zvi, Israel
mno146@gmail.com
www.engelo.com/mno-home

Aimee Mitchell
6119 176th Street
Surrey, BC, Canada V3S 4E8
aimeezartz@gmail.com
www.etsy.com/shop/AimeezArtz
http://aimeezartz.blogspot.com/
page 83, 156 (Artist profile)

Damaris Oakley
2436 Cosgrove Crescent,
Vancouver Island, B.C., Canada
damaris@redfireart.com
www.redfireart.com

Isabella Raven
Raven's Curiosities
23 Savoy Rd.
Florida, MA 01247
isabellarvn@yahoo.com
www.RavensCuriosities.etsy.com
page 163 (Artist profile)

Kristy Sly
Kristy Sly Glass
14 N. Fourth St.
Madison, WI 53704
www.kristyslyglass.com
page 29, 158 (Artist profile)

Celeste Anne Strickland
Bathurst, South Africa
www.sunshinecrafts.etsy.com

Laura Tarbutton
LTDesign
110 Country Drive
Brandon, MS 39042
lauratarbutton@comcast.net
www.lauratarbutton.etsy.com
page 159 (Artist profile)

Index

ABOUT THE AUTHOR

Cecilia Cohen

GLASS & LIGHT, ISRAEL
WWW.GLASSANDLIGHT.BLOGSPOT.COM
WWW.GLASSANDLIGHT.ETSY.COM
WWW.STRINGYTHINGY.ETSY.COM

Cecilia Cohen is an artist, writer, and teacher. Her past includes an eclectic combination of professions—beekeeper, safety engineer, Webmaster, factory drone, housepainter, and camp counselor—and crafty pastimes that together have formed the creative foundation of everything she does today.

Her first studio was a worktable in her bedroom—with her mattress stuffed underneath—proving that if a person is determined enough, he or she will set up shop no matter how small a space they must contend with. Today, Cecilia has dedicated studio space, well lit and spacious, offering a view of her garden.

"My pride and joy is probably my glass storage unit, which I designed myself and had made to order by a local carpenter," she says. "Because I work with so many techniques and so many different kinds of glass, proper glass storage is critical. Another bit of studio furniture that I love is my lampworking table; I spotted a metal frame in a junkyard, brought it home, and cut a large piece of plywood to fit the top. The frame was originally the base of a choir's stage set. It's vaguely shaped like an *L*, generously sized, and strong enough to stand on—in fact, it can probably hold six to eight sopranos!"

Following the tradition of many artists, Cecilia is slowly taking over the rest of the house; her kilns are in her kitchen, and she has a home office where she writes books and tutorials, prepares study materials for her students, and stores yarns, fabric, embroidery threads, huge amounts of bubble wrap, and everything else she needs to manage her business.

ABOUT THE PHOTOGRAPHER

Nataly Cohen Kadosh

WWW.KADOSHNATALY.BLOGSPOT.COM

Nataly Cohen Kadosh graduated from Sapir College of the Negev in 1997, with a degree in television and film. She polished her photography skills as a photojournalist until 2002, when she opened her own business as a freelance photographer. Her work has taken her everywhere in Israel; she particularly enjoys the challenge of architectural and industrial photography, where one shot must often communicate a complete business concept.

Her love of image, texture, and color brings a process of discovery into the art of studio photography. "When I start a photography shoot," she notes, "I'm never quite sure what the final product will be—there are always surprises."

Nataly resides with her family in the desert town of Metar, in southern Israel. Her hobbies include architectural design, which she put to good use when she and her husband designed and built their family home with a full-size photography studio for her on the roof.